Contents

Introduction 1

Year one topics

Chapter 1: Utilitarianism 4

Chapter 2: Kantian Ethics 26

Chapter 3: Natural Moral Law 45

Chapter 4: Situation Ethics 62

Chapter 5: Euthanasia 80

Chapter 6: Business Ethics 101

Year two topics

Chapter 7: Conscience 120

Chapter 8: Metaethics 136

Chapter 9: Sexual Ethics 154

Appendix 1: A-Level Religious Studies Essay Advice 175

Appendix 2: Evaluating how well an ethical theory applies to an ethical issue 177

Introduction

How do you make an ethical decision? The OCR Religious Studies A Level course component 'Religion and Ethics' (H573/02) explores different ways of doing so through four normative ethical theories. A normative ethical theory is a way of helping you making an ethical decision, as distinguished from 'descriptive ethics' which simply describes differences in morals and 'Metaethics' which focuses on the meanings of words such as 'good' and 'bad' rather than deciding what to do in an ethical situation. The four normative ethical theories covered in the OCR Religious Studies A Level course are Utilitarianism, Kantian Ethics, Natural Moral Law (NML), and Situation Ethics. All four differ significantly from one another. Utilitarianism and Situation Ethics are teleological (where the end justifies the means) and relativistic (what counts as the right action varies depending upon the situation). Kantian Ethics and NML are absolutist (where the right action does not vary according to the situation). Kantian Ethics is deontological (ruled-governed). NML is deontological, but what makes the rules correct are that they are teleologically-oriented insofar as the rules promote human flourishing. NML is the only normative ethical theory featured in the OCR course which is clearly founded on a religious basis, although Situation Ethics hints at as much in the centrality of the term *agape* (selfless love). Kantian Ethics refers to a God at the end of the theory almost as an add-on, but could otherwise work as a secular theory. Utilitarianism is explicitly secular, liberal, egalitarian and humanistic. The OCR course then asks you to apply these theories to three important ethical issues of Euthanasia (NML and Situation Ethics), Business Ethics (Kantian Ethics and Utilitarianism), and Sexual Ethics (all four theories). In addition to these subtopics, the OCR course allows you to explore Metaethics and also what we mean by the ide of Conscience, in particular allowing you to make links to NML through exploring Aquinas' views on the latter topic and contrasting them with Sigmund Freud's.

This book functions as a study guide to help navigate through this component of the course. It covers all nine sections of the OCR A Level Ethics component. The chapters are all structured identically. Each chapter starts with a revision summary which includes capsule-like summarises of essential information such as key word lists, scholar lists, quotes, and possible questions. Each chapter then includes a brief theoretical summary of core 'Assessment Objective 1' (AO1) content to do with knowledge and understanding, written longhand. The chapters then move on to discuss in paragraph form each of the 'issues arising from' mentioned in the specification, bringing in other scholars where appropriate. Each chapter then finishes with a sample essay written in an examination style. At the end of the book there is some guidance on how to answer examination questions and apply theories.

Chapter 1: Utilitarianism

Revision Summary: Utilitarianism

Key Terms
- Principle of Utility
- Hedonism
- Hedonic Calculus
- Classical Utilitarianism
- Higher and Lower Pleasures
- Competent judge
- Universalisability
- Teleological
- Preferences
- Strong Rule Utilitarianism
- Weak Rule Utilitarianism
- 'Rule of thumb'

Documents:
Introduction to the Principles of Morals and Legislation (Bentham)
Utilitarianism (Mill)

Scholars' names
Jeremy Bentham, John Stuart Mill, Henry Sidgwick, Peter Singer, R. M. Hare, Richard Brandt
Influenced: W. D. Ross
Critics: Bernard Williams, Philippa Foot, Roger Crisp, G. E. Moore

Useful quotations
'Pushpin is as good as poetry' (Bentham)
'It is better to be a human being dissatisfied than a pig satisfied' (Mill)
'It is better to be Socrates dissatisfied than a fool satisfied' (Mill)
'Equal preferences count equally whatever their content' (R. M. Hare)
'Our own preferences cannot count any more than the preferences of others' (Peter Singer)

Curriculum links
Situation Ethics (a contrasting teleological approach)
Kant (an opposing deontological approach)
Business Ethics
Sexual Ethics (Reproduction)
Euthanasia
Metaethics

Stock strengths of Utilitarianism
- People do often decide what is right and wrong based on maximising good consequences.
- It has universal appeal – it doesn't depend on any religious belief but uses a simple observation of what human beings want from life.
- It is egalitarian. Everyone is worth the same.
- It is flexible – it can adjust to suit changing times. (As we understand animal pain better, we can change laws to reflect this).

Stock weaknesses of Utilitarianism

- It is impossible be sure of the consequences (saving a drowning boy who grows up to be Hitler).
- It does not take into account intentions.
- What's better: quality or quantity of pleasure (Haydn and the Oyster case)?
- Minorities can be exploited by the majority (Bernard Williams' 'Jim and the Indians' case).
- It requires you to ignore special relationships (should you donate a kidney to your mother or a more needy stranger? What about W.D. Ross' ethics as an alternative?).
- It can allow for evil means to justify good ends (torturing the innocent child of a terrorist to find a bomb).

Possible questions

To what extent does Utilitarianism provide a helpful method of decision-making? (40 marks)

How far can an ethical judgement about something being good, bad, right or wrong be based on the extent to which, in any given situation, utility is best served? (40 marks)

To what extent is it possible to measure good or pleasure and then reach a moral decision? (40 marks)

Utilitarianism further reading

An excellent link to a wealth of Utilitarianism resources and original texts
https://www.utilitarianism.com/index.htm

IEP
https://www.iep.utm.edu/util-a-r/

Stanford Encyclopaedia
https://plato.stanford.edu/entries/utilitarianism-history/

Utilitarianism: a brief summary

Jeremy Bentham (1748-1832) was an English philosopher and reformer. Following ancient Greeks such as Epicurus and the Scottish philosopher David Hume, Bentham thought humans were motivated by pursuing pleasure and avoiding pain. This is an idea known as 'hedonism.' In his *Introduction to the Principles of Morals and Legislation*, Bentham referred to this as humans being 'governed' by the 'two sovereign masters,' pleasure and pain. Using this semantic field of governance, Bentham thought that humans try to- and should- pursue pleasure and avoid pain in all that we do, whether we admit to it or not. After grounding his hedonism in human nature in this way (psychological hedonism), Bentham had to come up with a means within his normative system of ethics to promote the 'greatest happiness,' by which he understood the aggregate of pleasure minus pain for all parties concerned. Bentham made it clear in the opening of the above-mentioned book that he considered pleasure as synonymous with happiness. Bentham's normative aesthetic was that 'more' equals 'better,' and so he is known as having taken a 'quantitative' approach to pleasure; the more happiness an act brings (the net balance of pleasure minus pain), the morally better it is. As such, Bentham's Utilitarianism is often referred to as 'Act' Utilitarianism as each act should be judged individually – using the Hedonic Calculus with seven points (intensity, duration, certainty, nearness, fecundity, purity, extent)—according to the principle of utility to maximise happiness. Confusingly, Bentham thought that for most day-to-day activities we partake in, such as brushing your teeth or making breakfast, you can go by a 'rule of thumb,' i.e., what essentially works. However, when we are confronted by a moral dilemma, we should use the hedonic calculus to establish what we should be doing. Whether using the rule of thumb or the Hedonic Calculus, Bentham's Utilitarianism is teleological, with the end justifying the means, and it is relativistic for what counts as the 'right action' in a situation will vary.

John Stuart Mill (1806-1873) was Bentham's godson, the son of Bentham's friend James Mill. The elder Mill was a member of the East Indian Company and was a historian. The younger Mill's education was an idiosyncratic experiment of sorts devised by his father and godfather. Famously hothoused from a very young age with an especial emphasis on the classical languages and works, Mill suffered a nervous breakdown during his early adulthood. Recovering by reading poetry, this experience helped shape his own version of Utilitarianism published in a book of that name which in fact was a compendium of serialised articles. For Mill, bodily pleasures that we share with other animals (sex, satisfying hunger) are less valuable than intellectual pleasures that are uniquely human (intellectual curiosity, appreciation of art). Famously, Mill wrote 'Better Socrates dissatisfied than a pig satisfied." Therefore, Mill takes a 'qualitative' approach to pleasure as some pleasure is of a higher quality than others; a 'competent judge' who has appreciated both values the higher more. This distinguishes Mill from his godfather, for Bentham thought that 'pushpin [a simple game] is as good as poetry.' Also, unlike Bentham, Mill is often referred to as a 'Weak Rule' Utilitarian as he thinks that most of the time we should conform our moral decisions to general rules, such as truth telling or not stealing, as these rules mostly promote the greatest happiness for the greatest number of people. These rules can be broken when it is obvious that it would promote the greatest happiness to do so, and here one would revert to the Hedonic Calculus to establish how to proceed. By contrast, a 'Strong Rule' Utilitarian would not break these rules. J. C. C. Smart contended that Strong Rule Utilitarianism goes against the teleological spirit of Utilitarianism, while Weak Rule Utilitarianism collapses back into Act Utilitarianism since one would frequently be raising the question about whether breaking the rule would be preferable to keeping it, resulting in calculations taking place after all in each contentious moral case. It is sometimes said that Mill differed from Bentham in a further way insofar as the former thought happiness was valuable, while the latter thought pleasure was valuable. In fact, Bentham thought happiness and pleasure were synonymous, while Mill was still a hedonist as he makes it clear that humans achieve happiness through pursuing pleasures (higher ideally). Nevertheless, Roger Crisp has accused Mill of being an 'inconsistent hedonist' for surreptitiously introducing another absolute value (intellectual stimulation) alongside pleasure.

In the twentieth century R. M. Hare (1919-2002) and his student Peter Singer (1946-) developed Preference Utilitarianism. Preference Utilitarianism aims to maximise not pleasure or happiness, but the preferences of those involved in an ethical situation. This development has come from a recognition that humans do not always pursue pleasure and avoid pain. Take marathon running or boxing. Even for successful, well-known participants, these sports result in more pain than pleasure. Hedonists such as Bentham and Mill would have to contort themselves in knots trying to explain how the likes of Paula Radcliffe or Mike Tyson have derived more pleasure than pain from their sports, but Preference Utilitarians can simply say that despite the greater amount of pain they have endured, running marathons and boxing is what they have preferred to do over other pursuits. If you are informed, know about the consequences, and it is genuinely what you want to do (rather than being coerced into doing it, which is Richard Brandt's concern), then it is better to give people what they prefer than what would make them happy (in hedonistic terms). Preference Utilitarianism is egalitarian, for Hare wrote 'Equal preferences count equally whatever their content,' while Peter Singer stated that 'our own preferences cannot count any more than the preferences of others.' The only other constraints are that Singer thought we should be 'impartial spectators,' looking at all preferences in a situation. Hare said we should 'step into someone else's shoes' to appreciate their preference. Unless you were a masochist, this kind of unbiased reciprocity should prevent someone (or a group of people) willingly preferring activities which harm other people. Unlike most normative ethical thinkers, Singer has included sentient animals in his ethical theory, for we should include their preferences when judging what is the best thing to do for all beings involved in a situation. While Singer's theory avoids the clear 'speciesism' (to use Singer's term) of Mill's theory which distinguishes between humans and pigs, Bentham was also mindful of the welfare of animals for he thought that as animals can 'suffer,' it was not morally important that they could not talk or think like human beings can.

Issues raised by Utilitarianism

Whether or not utilitarianism provides a helpful method of moral decision-making

Whether Utilitarianism constitutes a 'helpful' theory of moral decision-making very much depends on what we mean by 'helpful.' This rather predictable, analytical response to this issue is not so glib as it first appears, not least because what people want from an ethical theory differs so much. What I would want from an ethical theory is something which allowed me to make clear, timely decisions. Here is where Utilitarianism can fall down, and a thought-experiment can illustrate why. Philippa Foot's famous 'Trolley Dilemma' shows the limitations of Utilitarianism regarding both clarity and timeliness. If you (as a bystander) see five people strapped down to a track with a runaway train coming towards them, do you pull a lever in front of you to divert the train onto a side-track to run over one person strapped down to the track? According to Act Utilitarian basic mathematics, the answer should be clear in the numerical sense that the 'extent' of people concerned and the 'fecundity' of the future pleasures of the five over the one means you should pull the lever and save the five at the expense of the one. So far, so easy and helpful according to my twin criteria of 'clear' and 'timely.' However, people are more than numbers, at the very least in the non-trivial sense of having ages, health statuses, relationships and more besides. What if the five people strapped down to the one track were all one-hundred years old, while the one person on the other track happened to be a new-born baby? Again, this might seem to be a relatively straightforward calculation, this time in favour of saving the one person at the expense of the five. However, what if the people looked similar from a distance, but there were nagging doubts that the one person on the track was special in some way, perhaps recognising him as a famous medical scientist but that you were not sure. The lack of certainty (and method for obtaining certainty in a time-sensitive situation) would make it hard for a moral agent to make the correct ethical decision; by the time you had divined the identities of the people involved (if at all possible) and all the ramifications of the two alternatives (again, if this was at all possible), then the train would already have hit the five people. What this tells us is that Utilitarianism is not a helpful method of moral decision-making in time-pressured, ambiguous situations. However, this does not mean it is a poor method of moral decision-making where the moral agent has more time to deliberate. This raises the bigger issue of whether a moral agent would be justified in using different methods of ethical decision-making for different kinds of situation. Earlier I mentioned that the criteria I selected for what constituted a 'helpful' moral decision were 'clear' and 'timely.' However, if by 'helpful' one understood it to mean 'flexible,' then Act Utilitarianism and Weak Rule Utilitarianism would meet this criterion, although Strong Rule Utilitarianism would not be. Of course, there could well be other criteria for what counts as 'helpful,' and then it would be a matter of thinking through the different aspects of the theory in relation to the criteria, using scholars, examples, and reasoning to help.

Whether or not an ethical judgement about something being good, bad, right or wrong can be based on the extent to which, in any given situation, utility is best served

How one addresses this issue depends upon the type of Utilitarianism under consideration, the 'Classical' Utilitarians (Bentham and Mill) would have understood utility in hedonistic terms, whereas Singer and Hare would have understood utility as maximising preferences. For the Classical Utilitarians, one issue is the extent to which pleasure can be measured (see the next issue below for more of a discussion about this). It is also worth taking into consideration the relatively fringe Utilitarian view, 'Strong Rule,' which would involve an ethical judgement being good or right based on the exercise of the rule, rather than on utility being maximised in each situation; it could be that utility could be better served by breaking the rule in a given situation (such as Bonhoeffer being involved in a plot to assassinate Hitler), but the rule of refraining from murdering people would be broken. This issue also invites comparison with other ethical theories. Natural Moral Law (NML) would hold that an ethical judgement depends upon not whether utility is best served, but on whether an action involves pursuing a 'real good,' in other words a good which helps a human being flourish according to their God-given purpose having been made in his image. Chasing pleasure or maximising preferences would be seen by followers of

NML as chasing an 'apparent good.' Followers of Kantian Ethics would certainly disagree that judgements about the right and the good can be based on the extent to which utility is best served in any given situation. They would argue for a deontological position in which what is right is following your duty, and that the only intrinsically good thing is a 'good will' (a will which follows duty for duty's sake). Situation Ethics is another ethical theory which, while being similarly teleological and relativistic to Utilitarianism, would hold that what is right is maximising not utility, but *agape*; what is right is the most loving thing to do, not what will bring about the most pleasure. However, while Situation Ethics appears different in this regard to Utilitarianism, when you drill-down into what *agape* means, it appears that it is self-sacrificial, other-regarding love. While this is certainly different to hedonistic utility, it is not so far away from utility couched in Preference Utilitarian language. This is especially so if one 'steps into someone else's shoes' and decides that what is best to do is to follow someone else's preference, even if it is as the expense of your own. A further way to approach this issue is to draw upon W. D. Ross' distinction between the 'right' and the 'good.' 'Rightness,' for Ross, indicated a deontological approach to moral issues, such as Kant's. 'Good,' though, for Ross pointed towards a range of intrinsic goods: pleasure, knowledge, virtue, and justice. Classical Utilitarianism is narrow insofar as it reduces goodness to the first of these four, pleasure. As such, utility would be maximising pleasure. Arguably, Mill is more nuanced since he also identifies 'knowledge' as an important 'higher pleasure.'

As for 'virtue' and 'justice,' here is where Utilitarianism can be see as lacking. For Utilitarianism, the locus of goodness is found in the consequences of an action, not in the person, thus neglecting one of the most ancient ethical traditions found in the works of Aristotle and in modern virtue theorists, such as Hursthouse, MacIntyre, and Anscombe. As for 'justice,' Foot's 'Trolley Dilemma' mentioned above – along with her other similar dilemmas such as the 'Fat Man' and 'Surgeon' dilemmas- also highlight what is for me the greatest problem with Utilitarianism and that is its lack of justice for minorities. By 'minorities' I am not talking in the demographic sense (although at the level of policy this could be the case if legislation was drawn up on using Utilitarian principles), but those in the numerical minority. If Utilitarianism is meant to promote utility in the sense of creating 'the greatest happiness for the greatest number of people,' then what happens to the happiness of the 'smallest number of people' — can they be at best ignored, or at worst steamrollered, in the interest of serving the majority? If so, this would make me reticent in identifying an ethical judgement about what is 'good' with the extent to which utility can be best served.

Whether or not it is possible to measure good or pleasure and then reach a moral decision

Through his 'Hedonic Calculus,' Bentham tried to measure pleasure and then reach a moral decision. With its seven criteria—Intensity, Duration, Certainty, Nearness, Fecundity, Purity, and Extent—the Hedonic Calculus was meant to be an objective measure by which to measure the amount of pleasure likely to be derived from a course of action. Intensity means how much you 'feel' the pleasure. Duration is how long the pleasure will last. Certainty is how likely it is to occur. Nearness is how long you would need to wait for it to happen. Fecundity is how fruitful the pleasure is likely to be; will it give rise to future pleasures? Purity is how much the pleasure will be mixed with pain. Extent means how many people will be affected by the pleasure. Indeed, this final criterion helps allay the surprisingly commonly held fear that Utilitarianism is a selfish ethical theory. Indeed, the nineteenth-century essayist Thomas Carlyle unfairly characterised Bentham's Utilitarianism as a 'philosophy of swine.' Pigs are said (also unfairly) to be selfish and greedy. While I think Bentham's theory gets around the 'selfish' connotation of 'swine,' arguably the 'greedy' aspect of Carlyle's criticism hits the mark, for looking at the issue in question it could be held that it might be possible to measure good or pleasure and then reach a decision calculated to maximise your own pleasure and/or that of others, but that this is not a moral decision because 'the good' should not be identified with gain, but other loftier concepts such as 'justice' or '*agape.*' Bentham would have countered that talk of this sort would be dealing with 'sounds instead of sense.' Nevertheless, Mill was wounded enough by Carlyle's snipe at Bentham to continue the porcine theme in his defence of his godfather by talking about satisfied pigs. Mill shifted the emphasis from the quantity of pleasure to its quality to get around the 'greed' angle, arguing humans were cut-out for more elevated things of an intellectual nature. Of course, the more obvious angle to take when attacking Bentham is questioning the extent to which it is possible to measure pleasure at all. I can measure a human's height in feet and inches or metres and centimetres. I can measure a human's weight in pounds and stone or grams and kilograms. However, there is no universally accepted, empirically-verifiable, objective unit for measuring pleasure. Nevertheless, it could be argued that pleasure is as physical a property of an individual as their height or weight, and it could be measured through taking blood draws and looking at serotonin levels. While this is possible, this would be both deeply impractical and problematic for making a moral decision. Theoretically, a society could be set up on Utilitarian lines with a database of typical serotonin levels reported on the performance of a vast array of actions helping inform a moral agent deciding upon different possible courses of action. There would be numerous problems in this far-fetched scenario. One problem would be that no two situations are exactly the same; if high serotonin levels were recorded from action X, this occurred in situation A; if action X occurs in situation B, then there could be other factors extraneous to the action which contributed to the serotonin levels experienced by the individual(s) affected. Here is the other principal problem with measuring pleasure, and that is that the individuals are just that: individuals. There is significant subjectivity in the response of individuals to stimuli. One person might love X, another person might hate it. This is not the case with height; regardless of an individual's preference, someone's height is their height. As such, even measuring serotonin levels and basing decisions from typical responses is fraught with problems, making Utilitarianism an unreliable decision-making tool in at least its Act Utilitarian version.

Sample essay

To what extent, if any, is Utilitarianism a good theory for approaching moral decisions in life? (40 marks)

Utilitarianism is a teleological, relativistic normative ethical theory which aims to create the greatest possible outcome for the greatest number of people, whether that be creating the maximum amount of pleasure (Bentham), happiness (Mill) or satisfaction of preferences (Hare and Singer). Due to the uncertainty of consequences and lack of justice for minorities, I will be arguing that Utilitarianism is not a good theory for approaching moral decisions in life.

My view, rightly, is that there are significant problem with Utilitarianism—and any moral teleological theory—in that it is implausible to think that moral agents can calculate consequences with accuracy. Take Philippa Foot's 'surgeon dilemma.' On the surface of things, it seems right on Utilitarian principles to kill one healthy person to save five people otherwise certain to die, for you would be increasing for the five saved patients what Bentham would have regarded, according to his Hedonic Calculus, as being 'fecundity' (chance of future pleasures), 'extent' (five people rather than one) and the 'duration' of pleasure for the five able to live. However, does one stop calculating at the seven people immediately involved in the situation (surgeon, healthy person, and five unhealthy people) or their families? Should they be taken into consideration with 'extent,' or not? If the moral situation is extended to them, why not widen 'extent' to include all potential patients in the future who might be reluctant to visit a doctor's surgery for a check-up if news got out about what the surgeon has done? This could cause great 'impurity' in the future, with more pain to arise than pleasure. The lack of clarity about where one should stop calculating affects whether the moral decision is to kill the one healthy person is right or wrong, making Utilitarianism an implausible, bad theory for approaching moral decisions in life. Some Utilitarians, such as Mill, would wrongly reply that 'Rule Utilitarianism' gets around this problem as if you have a rule which generally maximises pleasure or happiness—such as 'Do not kill innocent people'—then this would eliminate any uncertainty about the right course of action as one is no longer required to calculate uncertain future consequences, making Utilitarianism a good theory for approaching moral decisions in life. My view is more convincing as Rule Utilitarianism is not immune from the problem of calculating consequences. J. C. C. Smart has said that this is because Rule Utilitarianism either collapses into Act Utilitarianism (using the Hedonic Calculus) because one is trying to calculate whether one is confronted with an exception to the rule which allows it to be broken (and here we are back with the difficulty of calculating consequences), or it does not allow exceptions to the rule and then there are better, more robust and sophisticated deontological alternatives to Strong Rule Utilitarianism such as Kantian Ethics which give more guidance for establishing rules in the first place, such as

Kant's Categorical Imperative with its emphasis on universalisability and not using someone as a means to an end. As both Act and Rule Utilitarianism struggle to deal with calculating consequences, Utilitarianism is not a good theory for approaching moral decisions in life.

My view, rightly, is that Utilitarianism is not a good theory for approaching moral decisions in life as it is unjust because it exploits minorities. This is because of Bentham's 'greatest happiness principle,' essentially meaning that in moral decision-making, the right action is that which creates 'the greatest happiness for the greatest number of people.' What, then, about the 'smallest number' involved? Like the surgeon dilemma, Philippa Foot's even more famous 'Trolley Dilemma' highlights this problem well. If a trolley is out of control, hurtling down a track, the logical thing to do when considering 'extent,' 'fecundity' and 'purity' is to pull a lever, diverting the trolley from hitting five people by instead making it hit one person. This seems unfair on the one person. Such a dilemma exists in real life when making policy decisions: with finite, limited resources, do you help the majority at the expense of the minority? Neglecting the minority seems unfair. Wrongly, some more modern Preference Utilitarians would disagree with this criticism of Utilitarianism, saying that it depends upon a 'maximising' approach to happiness, with the more pleasure created, the better. Instead, Hare would say we need to 'step into someone else's shoes' when considering different preferences in a situation. In the trolley dilemma, one should imagine how the one person who will be run over by the trolley would feel and what their preference would be in the situation, and vice-versa. As such, it is less likely that minorities (numerical or interest group) would be exploited by Preference Utilitarianism compared with the Classical Utilitarianism of Bentham. My view is more compelling because Preference Utilitarianism falls foul of similar objection to Classical Utilitarianism. This becomes apparent when, again, considering the trolley dilemma, for if the person in control of the lever has to put himself in the shoes of the one person on the other track, he also needs to put himself in the shoes of the five people about to be run over on the main track; it is very likely they would want you to pull the lever, even after putting themselves in the shoes of both you and the one person on the side track. This is because many humans are empathetic only to a degree; David Hume talked of 'limited altruism,' and one is much more likely to feel strongly about one's own preferences than other peoples', so when considering the aggregate of preferences, minorities are still likely to be exploited. Such lack of justice makes Utilitarianism a bad theory for approaching moral decisions.

On balance, Utilitarianism is a poor normative ethical theory when it comes to moral decision-making. This is because its teleological nature makes it difficult for moral agents to know the right thing to do as it contains no clearly-defined cut-off point for where one should stop calculating consequences. Moreover, it lacks justice for minorities as they will be seen as being in the 'smallest number,' whereas Utilitarianism prioritises making decisions for the 'greatest number.'

Chapter 2: Kantian Ethics

Revision Summary: Kantian Ethics

Key terms/ideas
- Autonomy
- A priori
- Heteronomy
- Deontological
- Hypothetical imperative
- Categorical imperative
- Immortality
- Postulate
- Kingdom of ends
- Universalisation
- Inclination
- Dignity
- Good will
- Summum bonum
- Phenomenal self
- Noumenal self
- Free will
- Absolute
- Reason
- Duty

Key scholars (for and against)
Kant, Nietzsche, Hegel, Mill, Anscombe, Aquinas, Schopenhauer, Scruton, Fletcher, Hume, Ross

Key documents
Critique of Pure Reason
Groundwork on the Metaphysics of Morals

Metaphysics of Morals
Critique of Practical Reason
Critique of Judgement

Quotes
'Life without reason and morality has no value' (Kant)
'Live your life though your every act were to become a universal law' (Kant)
'A good will is not good because of what it makes or accomplishes; it is good only through willing what is good in itself' (Kant)
'To have any goal or action whatsoever is an act of freedom on the part of the acting subject' (Kant) 'The good will shines forth like a precious jewel' (Kant)

Possible questions
'Kantian ethics provides a helpful method of moral decision-making'- discuss (40 marks)

'Can an ethical judgement about something being good, bad, right or wrong be based on the extent to which duty is best served?' (40 marks)

'Kantian ethics is too abstract to be applicable to practical moral decision-making'- discuss (40 marks)

'Kantian ethics is too reliant on reason so that it unduly rejects the importance of other factors, such as sympathy, empathy and love in moral decision-making' - discuss (40 marks)

Curriculum links
Christian moral principles
Situation Ethics
Business Ethics
Death and the afterlife
Utilitarianism
NML
Sexual Ethics
Plato
Conscience (Freud)
Bonhoeffer
Marx
Euthanasia

Stock strengths
- Kant's theory safeguards minorities from exploitation.
- Kant's theory is fair and consistent as it prioritises universalizability.
- Kant's theory is universally accessible due to it being based on reason.

Stock weaknesses
- Universalisability is 'empty formalism' (Hegel) as it gives you the structure of ethics, but no content (i.e., it doesn't tell us what to do or not to do).
- 'Can universalise anything' (Alasdair MacIntyre) — similar to Hegel's criticism.
- Duty: cold? Inhumane? Not everybody believes that duty is the best motive for action (e.g., Hume).
- Freud: maybe human beings are not as rational and autonomous as Kant thought as we have a subconscious mind.

- Augustine: our rationality is tainted by original sin.
- Marx: his belief in materialism (all there is happens to be the physical world) means there is no noumenal self, therefore no autonomy.

Further reading

https://www.iep.utm.edu/kantmeta/

https://plato.stanford.edu/entries/kant-moral/

http://www.bbc.co.uk/ethics/introduction/duty_1.shtml

https://books.google.co.uk/books?hl=en&lr=&id=jftGAgAAQBAJ&oi=fnd&pg=PA1&dq=kantian+ethics&ots=4yxe0b2qFZ&sig=c1ISLpbr-A54QcXRKo2Lnwl-yAY#v=onepage&q=kantian%20ethics&f=false

Kantian Ethics: a brief summary

Kant was an 18th century German philosopher, often regarded as the figure mostly clearly associated with the Enlightenment period of thought. The Enlightenment was the 'Age of Reason,' where philosophers thought thinking could lead us to what is right. As such, Kant thought that while we all possessed a 'phenomenal self' which expresses itself in inclinations to do things and is caught up in the physical realm which appears to us through our senses, we also possess a 'noumenal self' which goes beyond the phenomenal realm. Having this noumenal self allows us to make rational, autonomous (self-directed) moral decisions because it is not caught up in the phenomenal realm of cause and effect, of being subject to the universal physical laws of nature described by Isaac Newton.

According to Kant, the morally good man is the man of good will, and that the man of good will is the man who does his duty. An action, therefore, only has moral worth if it is done from duty. This makes clear what doing your duty does not involve: it has nothing to do with obeying your inclinations, serving your own interests, and is not estimated in terms of consequences. Thus far the structure of Kantian Ethics has only eliminated what duty is not, but it has not yet made clear what your duty is. Nevertheless, Kant has underscored that his theory is deontological in its nature; consequences are of no importance for Kant.

The second thing about this duty is that it must be of universal application, applicable to everyone irrespective of their situation. As such, it must appeal to that aspect of human nature, which is common to all humans, namely, reason. This duty, in other words, has to be of such a kind that to obey it is to exercise the rational faculty and not to obey it is to lapse into irrational confusion. In following this law, then, the human of good will is using their reason in a moral matter, and what they do is what every reasonable human would do in similar circumstance. On the other hand, making an irrational decision is against acting in obedience to your duty. For Kant, what is contradictory is immoral.

What, then, is this supreme principle of morality? What is this rule or law that the human of good will consciously or unconsciously recognises when they obey their duty? Kant calls it the Categorical Imperative. An imperative tells you which of your possible actions would be good, and it does this in the form of a command, expressed by the words 'I ought.' Kant gives three versions of the Categorical Imperative, the first of which reads thusly: I ought never to act except in such a way that I can also will that my maxim should become a universal law.

The Categorical Imperative is obeyed solely because what it commands is accepted as being good in itself, as being an intrinsic good. The action is carried out because of the very nature of the action itself and not because it is the means of achieving something else. Nor is consideration given to the possible consequences of the action. 'If you want to go to the cinema, buy a ticket' is a hypothetical imperative which is a command you give to yourself only if you want a particular outcome (it is a non-moral command which is driven by emotions rather than reason). The categorical equivalent, however, would read simply 'Buy a ticket.' It is a command that must be obeyed for its own sake and not for any other motive. All moral commands, says Kant, are of this type.

However, the most significant feature of the Categorical Imperative is the importance he placed on universalisability, of willing 'that my maxim should become a universal law' – as it is this, Kant tells us, that gives us the method of identifying those laws which have universal moral worth. In other words, the test we have been looking for, the test that will tell us what rules all of us should obey, is whether or not the rule in question can be universalized, or as Kant puts it in another formulation, whether I it is possible for me to will that it become a 'law of nature.' What I must discover is whether this rule can be consistently acted upon by all those in similar situations; and from here it is the consistency of the rule that is decisive.

Kant did not think everyone always acted rationally, for the inclinations are strong and can tempt people to act from non-moral motives. Furthermore, the wicked often prosper and the virtuous suffer. Even more troublingly, Kant did not think he could prove we had the noumenal self required to be an autonomous, rational self-legislator. For these reasons Kant put forward the idea of the *'summum bonum'* (highest good). He postulated (put forward) that there had to be a God to make the *summum bonum* and an immortal soul, so that after death the virtuous could get the happiness they did not receive in life. If this were not so, Kant thought, the universe would be irrational. Also, Kant postulated humans have free will to be moral.

Issues raised by Kantian Ethics

Whether or not Kantian ethics provides a helpful method of moral decision-making

As with Utilitarianism in Chapter 1, answering this question depends entirely on what you judge to be required for something to be a 'helpful method of moral decision-making.' If you choose 'consistency' as being your most important criterion for judging a method of moral decision-making as 'helpful,' then Kantian Ethics would be considered helpful due to the first formulation of the Categorical Imperative ('universalisability') as all judgements need to be made assuming that other moral agents will be following them. As its is a deontological theory, there is also the practical, time-saving aspect that you do not have to be up against the clock in time-sensitive situations weighing up consequences, a clear advantage on Utilitarianism. However, Kantian Ethics assumes all moral agents are rational and that their rationality expresses itself in the same way, which could undermine the 'consistency' apparent benefit of Kantian Ethics when it comes to the notion of the 'contradiction in the will.' There is also the issue of whether, even if every moral judgement should be knowable *a priori*, the moral agent in question has rationally worked-out what their duty is prior to being confronted with the ethical dilemma to which the maxim applies. If not, then the apparent 'time saving' benefit would not be a real benefit over a teleological approach such as Utilitarianism. One of the clear disadvantages of Kantian Ethics is that it is inflexible as it allows no exceptions to the moral law, meaning that if you thought that 'helpful' was synonymous with 'flexible,' Kantian Ethics would be regarded as unhelpful. The other major unhelpful disadvantage of Kantian Ethics is that of conflicting duties. If you have promised to keep someone safe but you must tell a lie in order to do so, then you have to break one of your duties. As you cannot appeal to consequences or emotions to identify which duty you should break, then Kantian Ethics is an unhelpful method of moral decision-making.

Whether or not an ethical judgement about something being good, bad, right or wrong can be based on the extent to which duty is best served
As with the way in which this kind of issue was addressed in Chapter 1, a lot of how you deal with this issue as it applies to Kantian Ethics is dependent upon how you define 'good' or 'bad.' If you follow Kantian Ethics and its understanding of the only thing which shines forth as a 'precious jewel' (the only intrinsically good thing) to be a 'good will,' then you will regard serving duty as equivalent to doing something good and making the right ethical judgement. However, there are good reasons to doubt Kant's contention on this matter. A good will is a will which does duty for duty's sake and for no other motive. There are two ways to attack this notion. The first is the implausibility of an action being good if it results in terrible consequences. Imagine if someone consistently did their duty for duty's sake- cultivating a good will- and this involved telling the truth which resulted in the deaths of thousands of people. While Kant would contend that

the person has cultivated a good will, instinctively most people would see Kant's claim as implausible, divorced from the reality of suffering experienced by thousands of people; Bentham would have been top of the queue of doubters of Kant on this matter for reasons given in Chapter 1. The other way to attack Kant's understanding of the good will here is the idea that no other motive is intrinsically good. Joseph Fletcher would have had something to say about this through his contention that *agape* (selfless love to the point of being self-sacrificial) is the only intrinsically good thing. Of course, at this point there are two competing claims about a sole intrinsically good thing. In Kant's case he is pointing to an intrinsically good motive, while Fletcher is pointing to an intrinsically good absolute value which is also a motive for action (as well as a yardstick for judging consequences). What you need to do is to evaluate these competing claims to see which is the most plausible. Below the surface of Kant's judgement one can find his assumptions that the moral law needs to be consistent and rational, that the moral law reflected the consistency and rationality of the laws of nature. In support of an attack on Kant one could draw upon changes in our understanding of the laws of nature for Einstein's Theory of Relativity has shown there are inconsistencies in the laws of nature, so why should there not be inconsistencies in the moral law; if going against your duty would reduce suffering and misery for thousands, would it not be better to abandon your duty? In which case, one would be back with something like a form of 'Weak Rule Utilitarianism' than Kantian Ethics, casting doubt on an ethical judgement about something being good, bad, right or wrong being based on the extent to which duty is best served. If one wanted to go all-out against Kant, then one could also draw upon the chief 'hermeneuticians of suspicion' (to borrow Ricoeur's term), Marx, Nietzsche, and Freud who all- for different, varied reasons- sewed doubt about the consistency, and extent, of human rationality (and its importance). As for Fletcher's competing claim, its problem comes from *agape* comes from it being used in different ways: is it an absolute value, a motive, or a yardstick by which to judge consequences? According to three of the Six Fundamental Principles, love wills your neighbour's good (whether you like them or not), love is the only absolute, and the end justifies the means. This means that love is a motivation, value, and teleological yardstick. This indicates that *agape* is at least an unclear concept, at worst an incoherent one.

Whether or not Kantian ethics is too abstract to be applicable to practical moral decision-making

Hegel famously said that Kant's Categorical Imperative is 'empty formalism.' By this he meant that it is a formula to be employed, but one lacking any substantial content. This has led to some commentators contending that Kant's theory is overly abstract, impractical and therefore should not be taken seriously as an ethical theory. I would argue that this grossly mischaracterises Kant's ethics. Onora O'Neill can be thanked for succinctly pointing out the error of this judgement. She contended that Kant's *Groundwork of a Metaphysics of Morals* is structured like a piece of medieval scholastic philosophical theology, starting with the form, then the matter, then the explanation, but that once read, the last section informs the previous, which informs the first. The *Groundwork* indeed starts with the form- universalisability- and then the matter, which is the formulation of humanity as an end in itself. Finally, it finishes with the explanation, the formulation of the 'Kingdom of Ends.' According to O'Neill, what this means read backwards in the light of having read all of it, is that humans have intrinsic value insofar as they are autonomous self-legislators. In other words, humans have value as they can set themselves laws. Due to this intrinsic value, they should not be treated merely as a means to an end, but as ends in themselves. This in turn restricts what you could rationally will. While some maxims are 'contradictions in the laws of nature' ('Always jump the queue' would eliminate the concept of queueing if universalised), an appreciation of the intrinsic value of rational humans would prevent 'contradictions in the will' ('Use prostitutes' would be a case in point as you are using someone solely as a means to the end of your own gratification). As such, Kant's ethics are not so abstract to be impractical in the sense of being empty formalism. Where they do fall down is not in lacking substance to rule guide your decision-making, but in its substance not ruling out the absurd. While MacIntyre was wrong to say you could universalise anything, you can universalise some absurdities such as 'Always shut the door.' This contradicts neither the will nor the law of nature, yet it seems curiously non-moral and one could envision people constantly shutting the door. As such, the lack of concrete guidance to steer your duty away from these absurdities is a weakness of Kantian Ethics.

Whether or not Kantian ethics is so reliant on reason that it unduly rejects the importance of other factors, such as sympathy, empathy and love in moral decision-making Kant was awoken from his 'dogmatic slumbers' by David Hume's philosophy, not least the emphasis he put on the 'sentiments' (emotions) in ethical decision-making. If you were a 'Hard Determinist' such as Ted Honderich, especially if you were a physicalist who thought we are all determined by the laws of nature, then you would support Kant in his opposition to Hume, for if we acted out of emotions which had a physical origin then we would be no more free than an apple falling off a tree and therefore we could not be given praise or blame for our actions. However, if you are not a determinist of this sort then there are good reasons to be wary of Kant's rejection of emotions. Kant seemed to view humans as robots. In his classic 'Axe man' dilemma, he thought the right thing to do would be to tell the truth to a murderous axe man who knocked at your door asking where your friend was hiding. Ross, by contrast, thought a *prima facie* duty of gratitude to your friend would place his welfare above the duty to tell the truth. As Kant has no hierarchy of duties based on contingent factors such as personal relationships, he prioritises cold reasoning above the warmth of emotions and relationships. This gets him into problems when duties conflict, such as if you had promised your fiend to keep him safe. Ross' concept of *prima facie* duties helps get him out of this problem which is insuperable for Kant. Of course, Fletcher would give significant importance to love (*agape*) for reasons explored in Chapter 4 and mentioned already in passing.

Sample essay

'Acting out of duty is the best way to make an ethical decision'- Discuss (40 marks)

Acting out of doing your duty is a deontological approach to ethical decision-making, where the intention and action are what makes an action right, rather than the consequences. This is a view held most famously by the philosopher Kant. I will be arguing that this is not the best way to make an ethical decision duty for two reasons, the first being conflicting duties and the second being that it is too cold.

My view, rightly, is that a deontological approach to ethical decision-making is not the best due to the impracticality of having to deal with situations in which you find conflicting duties. This is because if, like Kant, you thought that you should only do your duty for duty's sake, there is nothing else to appeal to in order to make an ethical decision, leaving you without a clear reason to act. Kant illustrated this issue himself through the 'Axe man' dilemma. If a notorious axe murderer came to your house and asked where your friend was, threatening to kill him, what should you do? There seems to be a conflict of duty between keeping your friend safe and telling the truth. Kant, wrongly, would reply that there is no conflict of duty as though you would have a duty to tell the truth and say you were harbouring him in your house. If you lied this would go against your duty to tell the truth as, according to the Categorical Imperative, it is a universal moral law to tell the truth as you would not want to be lied to and that lying goes against the respect you should show to other humans as rational self-legislators. My view is more convincing because Kant ignores the possibility that you have promised to keep your friend safe. Breaking a promise is of equal importance as telling the truth as breaking both would have been regarded by Kant as a 'contradiction in the law of nature,' for making a promise and breaking it would be cheapening the concept of promise-making in the first place. Kant has no way out of this problem. Even later attempts at trying to resolve this issue on deontological grounds, such as W. D. Ross' *prima facie* duties' fail, for they solve one problem- of conflicting duties- by creating another one, namely a lack of clarity over what is your duty in the first place. This is because one person might 'intuit' a duty of 'gratitude' to a friend, prioritising keeping them safe, whereas another person might intuit a duty of 'fidelity,' by which they could understand it to mean telling the truth. This lack of consistency is unclear and goes against the essence of Kant's thought. As such, there is no satisfactory way to resolve the impracticality of conflicting duties, meaning acting out of duty is not the best way to make an ethical decision.

My view, rightly, is that acting out of duty is not the best way to make an ethical decision as it is too cold and impersonal. As Kant thought the only good thin without qualification is a 'good will,' which does duty for duty's sake, acting out of any other motive, helping someone out of compassion would be seen as morally irrelevant, which seems counter-intuitive. David Hume said 'Reason is, and ought, to be a slave of the passions,' meaning that Hume realised that ethical actions are motivated by feelings, not reason. Kant wrongly disagreed and thought that any action motivated by feelings was morally irrelevant. Even if one helped somebody out of compassion, this would not make the action morally creditworthy. This is because feelings such as compassion belong to our 'phenomenal' self, meaning that they are subject to universal physical laws, are outside our control, and therefore we are not responsible for them meaning we cannot be praised or blamed for acting in accordance with them. My view is more convincing than Kant's because we have learned from philosophers since he was writing just how much pure reason of a 'noumenal' self is compromised by other aspects of our being. Freud highlighted how much of our decision making originates beyond our awareness in our subconscious parts of our mind, such as the 'Id' and 'Superego,' whereas Nietzsche thought there was no autonomous 'doer' behind the 'deed,' and that humans are a play of forces, shaped by culture, ideals, and circumstances. As it is more plausible to think humans act out of feelings, and if like Freud and Nietzsche the idea of 'pure reason' is undermined, it is wrong to think that acting out of cold, passionless duty is the best way to make an ethical decision as the ethical agent is unlikely to have the motivation required for the action to be carried out.

Although Kant thought that acting from pure, practical rationality was the only way for a genuinely ethical decision to take place, doing so is fraught with problems.

Not only can acting out of duty lead to the impractical confusion of conflicting duties, but also it can mean that the ethical agent is lacking motivation to act. Humans are driven by more than reason, if they are driven by reason at all, and so insights from Hume, Freud, and Kant cast doubt on a rational, duty-based approach to ethical decision-making being successful.

Chapter 3: Natural Moral Law

Revision Summary: Natural Moral Law (NML)

Key Terms
- Aquinas' four tiers of law (Eternal, Divine, Natural, Human)
- Primary precepts (WORLD)
- Secondary precepts
- Real and apparent goods
- Purpose/*telos*, and *eudaimonia*
- *Synderesis* principle ('Do good and avoid evil')
- Doctrine/principle of double effect
- Ius (relating to general principles and using your reason to adapt them to situations) and lex (following laws as a manual; more deontological and absolutist)
- Interior and exterior acts

Relevant Bible texts:
- *Synderesis*: 'love your neighbour as yourself' (Matt. 22) — link to divine law
- 'Love your lord thy God'- in relation to primary precept 'Worship God'
- Reproduction and divine law (be fruitful and multiply)
- Romans 2:15: law written 'on your hearts' (St. Paul): influence on Aquinas

Documents:
- *Summa Theologica* (Aquinas)

- *Theologiae Moralis* (1697) — a manualist interpretation
- Sermon on the Mount (divine law)
- 10 commandments (divine law)

Scholars' names
- Influences: Augustine, Aristotle, Stoics (in. Cicero)
- Aquinas
- Influenced: John Finnis
- Critics: Germain Grisez, Barth, Nietzsche, Hume, Moore

Possible Exam Questions
To what extent does natural law provide a helpful method of moral decision-making (40 marks)

How far can a judgement about something being good, bad, right or wrong can be based on its success or failure in achieving its *telos*? (40 marks)

'The universe as a whole is designed with a *telos*, and human nature has an orientation towards the good' — discuss (40 marks)

To what extent can doctrine of double effect can be used to justify an action, such as killing someone as an act of self-defence? (40 marks)

Useful quotations
'True law is right reason in accordance with nature' (Cicero)

'It's an application of reason for common good' (Aquinas)

Curriculum links
Situation Ethics

Knowledge of God's existence
Christian moral principles
Problem of Evil (Barth, Augustine)
Sexual Ethics (Reproduction)
Conscience (*synderesis*)
Euthanasia (preservation of life)
Gender and Society
Metaethics
Aristotle

Stock strengths of NML
- Anthony Kenny: the Doctrine of Double Effect must form a part of any rational system of morality.
- It is universal and accessible to all humans using their reason correctly, so it is fair.
- It is flexible as secondary precepts can be adapted to new times, places and cultures.

Stock weaknesses of NML
- It is over-reliant on reason: Augustine would have thought our reason too corrupt due to the Fall of humans in Genesis 3, so we should rely on God's grace; Karl Barth would have agreed as he thought we should rely on the Word of God instead.
- John Calvin: NML ignores importance of the Bible.
- Kai Neilsen: modern anthropology indicates there are many human natures, not one.

NML further reading
Internet Encyclopaedia of Philosophy:
https://www.iep.utm.edu/natlaw/

Stanford Encyclopaedia of Philosophy
https://plato.stanford.edu/entries/natural-law-ethics/
John Finnis' book:
https://books.google.co.uk/books?hl=en&lr=&id=1lRFHEI6JQoC&oi=fnd&pg=PP1&dq=natural+law&ots=GUMY7wubKx&sig=eexewMcO_H-7k1lcxhFh84OiUqE#v=onepage&q=natural%20law&f=false

NML: a brief summary

Natural Moral Law is an absolutist theory most associated with the philosophical theologian and Dominican friar, St Thomas Aquinas (1224 -1274). It relies on Aquinas' basic understanding that humans innately try to do good and to avoid evil in order to find fulfilment and happiness in life (the *Synderesis* Rule).

Following on from the *Synderesis* Rule, Natural Law is based on five primary precepts. These primary precepts are fundamental principles revealed to us by God giving human nature a purpose (*telos*) that anyone using their reason (thinking) could understand. They are: Worship God, Ordered society, Reproduce, Learn Defend the innocent. These form a useful acronym 'WORLD.'

Humans are then to use their reason to establish rules that will fulfil the requirements of the primary precepts. These rules are known as secondary precepts. These can be flexible to time and place (a relativistic element), although in practice NML has often been absolutised in training manuals for trainee priests after the Council of Trent until the 1960s. Some examples are: 'Do not murder' (this fulfils the primary precept of 'defending the innocent') and 'Do not abort the unborn' (this fulfils the primary precepts of 'defending the innocent' and of 'reproduce').

Aquinas thought we should use our reason to establish what we should or should not do. Reason helps us identify the primary precepts by reflecting on our human nature, as well as ascertaining how we can fulfil them. Misuse of reason can lead us to chase apparent goods (such as using artificial contraception) rather than real ones (having sex primarily for the purpose of reproducing). As God is omniscient, he knows our intentions when we are performing actions, and so our interior act (intention) should be good as well as our exterior act (what we in fact do). Take the film *Taxi Driver*, for instance. Although the protagonist Travis Bickle was lauded by the public for rescuing a young girl from a pimp and so 'defended the innocent,' his intention that day was to cause chaos; it was only because he could not get near his intended target (a politician) that he caused havoc by shooting the pimp and his accomplices. As such, Aquinas would not have thought Bickle did a good act. Intention is important as sometimes NML allows flexibility through the Doctrine of Double Effect: someone could abort a baby to save the life of a mother as the intention is to defend life; the good done has to be proportional to the resultant unintended harm. The intention ('interior act') has to be good, as does the action ('exterior act') for an act to be judged to be right.

Aquinas thought that NML did not contradict Divine Law (revealed through the Bible and Church); some people should rely on Divine Law if they cannot reason well. Nevertheless, NML is open to everyone, not just Christians. Both NML and Divine Law have their origins in the Eternal Law in the mind of God, which humans cannot access directly as God is transcendent and we are immanent.

Issue arising from NML

Whether or not natural law provides a helpful method of moral decision-making

A good part of whether NML provides a helpful method of moral decision-making depends upon the way in which you take NML. If you follow a 'manualist' approach to NML then you will benefit from certainty, clarity, and timeliness of judgement if you have spent the time learning the moral principles from priestly manuals. However, this kind of priestly training has receded since the 1960s due to changes made during Vatican II. Moreover, this is a rigid, inflexible and some would say outdated way of making moral judgements, making a manualist approach unhelpful in these respects. Moreover, the manualist approach flies in the face of the value Aquinas placed on human reason since it involves the lower faculty of memory rather than the higher cognitive faculties of analysis and evaluation. If one takes a Thomistic approach rather than a manualist one there is more ambiguity in terms of what one should do as a new situation might necessitate the derivation of a new secondary precept, but there is the benefit of greater flexibility to meet new challenges. For instance, in the case of the threat to life ('defend the innocent') from STIs, Pope Benedict XVI decreed that it was morally permissible for sex workers in developing countries to use artificial contraception when working if they needed this work to earn enough money to stay alive, even though this went against prior Catholic teaching against the use of artificial contraception in all circumstances because it went against the primary precept to reproduce. While this flexibility is helpful, it raises questions about how helpful the Thomistic approach is regarding who has the authority to change secondary precepts, when, and in what circumstances. Also, it raises the question about how far the primary precepts have a hierarchy (does preserving life always trump reproduction) or not?

Whether or not a judgement about something being good, bad, right or wrong can be based on its success or failure in achieving its *telos*

Existentialists (such as Sartre) and nihilists (such as Nietzsche and Vattimo) would disagree with the idea that humans have a *telos* at all, so it would be fruitless to make a moral judgement based on something we do not have. Nietzsche went back to the meaning of terms such as 'good' and 'bad' and 'evil' to point to a 'slave revolt in morals' in order to draw attention to the human origins of moral terms rather than them being embedded in human nature. Nietzsche thought we were living after the 'Death of God' and that we are no longer impressed with claims of a divine order. Vattimo was influenced by Nietzsche and took up

Nietzsche's note that there are 'no facts, only interpretations,' and so if there are no facts then there can be no objective purpose for humans. In his modern version of NML, John Finnis would dispute Nietzsche's view, arguing that humans can intuit what is right by reflecting on human nature and society, being able to derive a natural law from seven 'basic goods,' which are 'life, knowledge, sociability of friendship, play, aesthetic experience, practical reasonableness and religion.' There are nine elements of practical reason then required in relation to these seven basic goods. The problem is that the choice of basic goods seems arbitrary (Dawkins would argue with 'religion') and the practical reason elements seem unreasonable, such as not getting obsessed with a project (if this were the case, then would there ever have been breakthroughs in science and medicine?).

Whether or not the universe as a whole is designed with a *telos*, or human nature has an orientation towards the good

Existentialists (such as Sartre) and nihilists (such as Nietzsche and Vattimo) would disagree with the idea that humans have a *telos* at all. Furthermore, the ethicist Bernard Williams (in his book *Morality*) conceded that while human-made artefacts such as clocks clearly have a purpose (telling the time) and so judgements can be made about them ('it is a good clock' would make no sense if it could not keep the time), it is far from clear what a human *telos* is, if we have one at all. Williams notes not only is it arbitrary to make human intelligence the 'distinguishing mark of man [sic.]' as humans have other unique aspects to humans which are not given moral import, but also that even if it was, it is far from clear that humans have an orientation towards the good from intelligence. Humans can use intelligence as an instrumental good rather than something with moral import or motivation, for humans can use cunning in a Machiavellian way to get what they want for what are often considered 'bad' or 'evil' motives and purposes. Away from existentialists and postmodernists, Darwinists will see humans as essentially no different from animals which have no souls, no moral purpose, and we are only living to pass on our characteristics to the next generation through the process of natural selection. Augustine would argue that humans, while created good, are fallen with warped will and faulty reasoning after the Fall. Instead, we should be reliant upon God's grace rather than our reasoning in order to orient ourselves to the good.

Whether or not the doctrine of double effect can be used to justify an action, such as killing someone as an act of self-defence

The doctrine of double effect has its place in NML and allows for more flexibility, even for a manualist interpretation of NML. However, it is not a justification for anything and everything. An often-overlooked aspect of the doctrine of double effect is 'proportionality.' This allows some bad actions to take place and be morally permissible, but not all. One such action would be the abortion of an unborn baby if continuing with the pregnancy would threaten the life of the mother. The intention of the act would have to be good (saving the mother) and the exterior act would be saving the mother's life, with the double (secondary) effect being the death of the unborn child. The actions would be proportionate, the death of one life to save the life of another. The mother as alive, although with less potential as older, has more existing responsibilities. If continuing with the pregnancy would have meant the mother would have lived but would have been -say- paralysed rather than dead, then abortion would not be justified as the effects would not have been proportional (the death of the unborn child being a bad act out of proportion to the woman not being paralysed). The doctrine of double effect could be used to justify killing someone in self-defence if you could know with reasonably certainty that your assailant was trying to kill you and would have been able to do so had you not intervened.

Sample essay

Critically assess NML as an approach to moral decision making (40 marks)

Natural Moral Law (NML) is a deontological normative ethical theory which was created by Thomas Aquinas in the thirteenth century and is still used today by Catholics. Underlying the theory is the assumption that humans, through right use of reason, should be able to follow the basic *synderesis* rule of 'do good and avoid evil,' whether or not one has heard of the Divine Law of the Church, and even thought one cannot access the Eternal Law in the mind of God. Human Law should conform to NML because the latter helps humans fulfil their *telos*, to reach *eudaimonia*—eternal life with God—having fulfilled our potential. I believe NML is a poor approach because it does not take into account human diversity, it does not work in practice, it commits the naturalistic fallacy, and a teleological approach might be better.

My view, rightly, is that NML is implausible as an approach to moral decision-making as there is no agreed single human nature, so there should be a less monolithic approach to moral decision-making. Kai Neilsen said different cultures have different understandings of human nature, which leads away from NML to relativism. There might not be a fixed *telos* but instead culturally-relative understandings of what it means to be human so this would affect what people would decide to do ethically in relation to their nature. Nevertheless, Aquinas would have wrongly believed that differences in understanding of human *telos* result from irrationality; when one uses reason properly, it is clear what should lead to *eudaimonia* and so people will chase real goods, not the apparent ones which result from sinfulness and irrationality. My view is more convincing as it is not plausible that whole cultures could be irrational, only individuals, so perhaps relativism makes more sense, which would affect ethical decision-making. Vardy and Grosch in *The Puzzle of Ethics* said that Aquinas gives too simple a view of human nature (for example, that sexuality just about reproduction), and Bernard Williams has said that even if we agree with Aquinas that 'reason' is a distinguishing mark of being human, it could just as easily lead to subjectivism as to agreeing on a universal *telos* for human beings. If the fundamentals of human nature cannot be agreed upon, it cannot be the basis for consistent, reliable moral decision-making.

My view, rightly, is that NML is a poor approach to moral decision making because the Church has ossified the secondary precepts into absolute moral laws. For example, in the Catholic Church artificial forms of contraception, such as condoms, were declared to be an intrinsic evil according to Pope Paul VI's encyclical letter *Humanae vitae* in 1968, meaning there is a secondary precept not to use artificial contraception. This is because artificial contraception frustrates the primary precept of reproduction; the intention of using artificial contraception would be to prevent a life from being formed, which goes against our *telos*. Aquinas might wrongly argue that this is the problem of the Church in interpreting his teaching rather than in NML itself, for the whole idea of secondary precepts is that it introduces some flexibility and even—arguably—relativism into his theory, for while there are five absolute primary precepts which, objectively, derive from human nature, circumstances might change; in a time where STIs are prevalent, if the 'interior act' was to use artificial contraception to preserve innocent life if one's job was, for example, a sex worker because there was no other work available, then Aquinas might have seen artificial contraception as morally acceptable. Furthermore, in a time of overpopulation one might use reason to obtain the secondary precept 'reproduce responsibility' (such as having only one child), until the world's population has reached optimal levels. Nevertheless, my view is more convincing as NML is used almost exclusively by the Roman Catholic Church and it has become intertwined with Church authority to the extent that the magisterium (teaching) of the Catholic Church has supplanted the 'right use of reason' on pain of excommunication which means that, in practice, secondary precepts are as inflexible as primary ones.

My view, rightly, is that one can see limitations in the NML approach to moral decision-making insofar as absolutism at the level of primary precepts can cause insoluble conflicts between them. Take the primary precepts of 'order in society' and 'preserve innocent life.' The refugee crisis in Europe in the last decade has highlighted the conflict between these two precepts. Hundreds of thousands of migrants from Africa and the Middle East have flooded Europe, particularly Italy and Greece. Many of these migrants have been fleeing war, disease and famine. Insofar as humans are using the clear light of right reason, European citizens should derive, and follow the secondary precept 'provide asylum to refugees.' However, Europe is already densely populated and has been facing a time of political and economic hardship for the ten years following the financial crash. The world's population has doubled in the last half century, causing strain on the infrastructure of developed countries. As the rise of the far right across Europe, along with attacks and counter-attacks between refugees and right-wingers has shown, there has been a breakdown of 'order in society' due to this crisis. However, Aquinas might wrongly argue that far right extremists and economic conservatives have been pursuing the 'apparent goods' of nationalism and economic protectionism rather than promoting the 'real good' of preserving the lives of innocent refugees. Nevertheless, my view is more convincing as Aquinas was writing in a simpler age when there were not so many economic pressures which threaten the poorest in society caused by the influx of so many extra people, as Europe was under, rather than over, populated, and there was not the threat of terrorism that there is today.

Due to NML not only being so old, but also wedded to the Roman Catholic Church, it cannot be a good source of moral decision-making. It is based on an outmoded understanding of human nature which does not consider the increasing acknowledgment of cultural relativism and divergent rationalities which are the result of difference, not sin. Furthermore, because NML has become inextricably linked to Roman Catholic authority it has lost the flexibility it originally had within it, making it a poor way of dealing with modern moral problems such as contraception, overpopulation, and refugee crises.

Chapter 4: Situation Ethics

Situation Ethics: Revision Summary

Key terms/ideas
- Situationism
- Antinomianism
- Legalism
- Four Working Principles
- Personalism
- Positivism
- Pragmatism
- Relativism
- Six Fundamental Propositions
- *Agape*
- Absolutism
- *Philos*
- *Eros*
- Altruism
- Teleological

Key scholars
Joseph Fletcher, William Temple, John Robinson, Augustine, D.Z. Phillips, W.D. Ross, Anthony O'Hear

Key documents
Situation Ethics
Christianity and Social Order
Honest to God

Key quotes
'Love and justice are the same' (Fletcher)
'Only one 'thing' is intrinsically good; namely love' (Fletcher)
'God is love' (1 John 4)
'faith, hope and love abide…the greatest of these is love' (St. Paul, 1 Corinthians 13:13)

Key case studies
Patriotic Prostitution dilemma

Possible questions
To what extent does Situation Ethics provide a helpful method of decision-making? (40 marks)
'Ethical judgements about something being good, bad, right or wrong can be based on the extent to which, in any given situation, *agape* is best served'- discuss (40 marks)
To what extent is Situation Ethics religious? (40 marks)
'Situation Ethics is individualistic and subjective'- discuss (40 marks)

Curriculum links
- NML
- Utilitarianism
- Kant
- Christian Moral Principles
- Augustine
- Jesus Christ
- Metaethics
- Conscience

- Sexual Ethics
- Euthanasia

Stock strengths
- Flexible.
- Personal.
- Contemporary, but nonetheless with a strong tradition behind it.

Stock weaknesses
- Determining outcomes/flawed reason (Augustine, Barth).
- Are there not intrinsically evil actions? Anthony O'Hear: how could it ever possibly be right to throw babies onto bonfires?
- How can we ever be sure we have done the most loving thing? D. Z. Phillips says this moral knowledge is beyond us.
- D. Z. Phillips has also suggested that there's a difference between a 'right' action and a 'good' one. Killing a terrorist who is about to murder a child is the right action, but the destruction of a man's life is not a good thing.
- Unbiblical in its understanding of *agape*.

Further reading

https://www.christiancourier.com/articles/55-critical-look-at-situation-ethics-a

https://peped.org/philosophicalinvestigations/ethics/ethics-as/situation-ethics/

Situation Ethics: a brief summary

Joseph Fletcher (1905-1991) was an American ethicist whose most famous work was *Situation Ethics* (1966). Fletcher's intellectual journey was an interesting one, from ordained Episcopal priest to an atheist humanist to the point of being one named 'Humanist of the Year' in 1974 and being a signer of the Humanist Manifesto. Fletcher was a leading proponent of medical ethics and was not afraid to make academic contributions to controversial issues such as abortion, eugenics, and euthanasia. Despite being prolific, it is for *Situation Ethics* that he is best remembered today.

Situation Ethics has sometimes- unfairly- been dismissed for being a product of its time. Appearing in 1966, it has often been reduced to 'all you need is love,' to a cultural artefact of the hippie era, despite the fact that the song of that name did not appear until a year later; perhaps Lennon and McCartney had read *Situation Ethics*. What, though, did Fletcher mean by 'love'? Fletcher makes clear he was not thinking of *eros* (romantic love), *philos* (friendship love), *storge* (familial love), but *agape* (selfless love). *Agape* is sometimes referred to as selfless love and/or sacrificial love. While these two interpretations of this concept differ, they can be connected. When combined it could mean at the very least that one sacrifices one's own preference to promote the good of the other person(s) involved in the situation, although Fletcher took a teleological view of *agape* rather than seeing it as an attitude; it seems to Fletcher as though *agape* meant doing the best for the other in the situation rather than having an attitude of selfless concern for the other. Here, again, terminology is important, for Fletcher positioned his normative ethical theory as putting the 'situation' at the forefront, as the midway point between legalism (strict adherence to laws) and antinomianism (anarchy). In short, Situation Ethics is a teleological theory which tasks the moral agent of doing good for the other.

Underpinning Situation Ethics are six fundamental principles (sometimes called propositions):
1. Love is the only absolute (it is intrinsically good)
2. Christian decision making is based on love
3. Justice is love distributed
4. Love wants the good for anyone, whoever they are
5. Only the end justifies the means
6. Love is acted out situationally not prescriptively

These fundamental principles show that Situation Ethics is absolutist with regard to values, but not rules (principles 1 and 6), that it is teleological (principle 5), impartial (principle 4), has some connection to Christianity (principle 2), and reduces justice to relativism (principle 3). Regarding principle 3, it is also interesting to note that Fletcher thought that 'conscience' is a verb rather than a noun; it is something we do (distributing love is acting in a conscientious, just way) rather than something we have, unlike the views of thinkers such as Augustine or Newman.

How does one go about deciding what the most loving thing is? Here one can look to Situation Ethics' 'Four Working Principles':
1. Pragmatism
2. Relativism
3. Positivism
4. Personalism

The first working principle means that ethical decisions need to be practical and work in the real world and daily life. The second principle is that ethical decision-making has to be situational and avoid fixed moral rules. The third principle means that faith should be placed before reasoning and so- like a theologian- one should have faith, in this case about the need to maximise love: 'It is a choice, not a result reached by force of logic.' Personalism means that people should be put at the centre of ethical decision-making, not rules or any other locus of concern.

Issues arising from Situation Ethics

Whether or not situation ethics provides a helpful method of moral decision-making

There are three main ways of approaching this issue. They are to compare Situation Ethics with legalistic, antinomian, and other teleological approaches to moral decision-making. When compared with antinomian approaches to moral decision-making, Situation Ethics is more helpful insofar as it provides some guidance through both the Working Principles and Fundamental Propositions. For example, we know we should put people rather than rules (or anything else) at the centre of moral decision-making, and that we should keep the absolute value of *agape* in mind when making moral decisions. Guidance of this sort is helpful and informs you to avoid slavish obedience to laws or putting yourself first. This provides more guidance than antinomianism which provides no guidance at all. However, antinomianism might come more easily to people insofar as it allows them to do what they want, giving them the motivation to act, whereas ethical egoists such as David Hume would say that it is very hard (or even impossible) to act in a selfless way all the time, making Situation Ethics an unhelpful method of moral decision-making compared with antinomianism because if you cannot find the willpower to follow-through on your moral judgements then there is little point making the decisions in the first place. Compared with legalistic normative ethical theories such as Kantian Ethics and NML, Situation Ethics is less helpful insofar as it does not provide clear-cut rules to follow, meaning decision-making will likely be more time-consuming and ambiguous. Compared with Utilitarianism, another teleological normative ethical theory, Situation Ethics is less helpful in different ways. Compared with Act Utilitarianism it does not provide anything as specific as the Hedonic Calculus to give criteria against which to compare possible courses of action (even though it has the *agape* calculus). Compared with Rule Utilitarianism it does not provide a method of quick decision-making which does not require calculation of possible outcomes. Compared with Preference Utilitarianism it does not permit for actions to benefit the self primarily, thus it would be unhelpful to try to always act in an *agape*ic manner if your psychological makeup is not geared towards this way of making moral decisions.

Whether or not an ethical judgement about something being good, bad, right or wrong can be based on the extent to which, in any given situation, *agape* is best served

The fundamental principles are interesting, especially as they point to *agape* being used to refer to different things. *Agape* is an absolute value which is distributed in a relativistic way. However, to judge that the end justifies the means one needs to point towards the most loving thing to do, which is 'the good,' but how is the good to be understood? If one is meant to decide what to do based on love and if it is agapeic and so understood as being other-regarding, what one is meant to be doing is acting selflessly for someone else's good. However, if love is the absolute value, what is 'good' except love? This becomes somewhat tautological, unless the 'good' refers to something like the welfare of your neighbour, or their pleasure, or preference, or anything else which fills in the gap of 'good.' As such, it is difficult to say whether even from the perspective of Situation Ethics, an ethical decision can be justified solely with reference to *agape* if it is implicit in the structure of the theory that 'good' is ambiguous. As with any issue of worded in such a way, a question asking you to explore this issue invites comparisons with other ethical theories. Of course, if you bring in other theories to answer a question like this in an A Level essay then the focus should be on the named theory with other theories being used to highlight strengths and/or weaknesses of the theory under consideration; as such, I would not recommend having free-standing paragraphs on the other theories. As already mentioned, Utilitarians would identify good with pleasure or satisfaction of preferences and a right action to be one maximising the good for the greatest number of people concerned. Kant would identify the good with a good will, and a right action would be one which performs your duty for duty's sake. NML would identify the good with fulfilment of your *telos* and a right action would be following a rule which promotes the fulfilment of your *telos* (a secondary precept). The harder task in writing an essay on a question based on this issue arising from Situation Ethics is to move beyond simply comparing Situation Ethics with one or more other theories but instead to make a judgement about which has a better 'fundamental.' For instance, Situation Ethics' 'fundamental' of *'agape'* could be argued to be better than Classical Utilitarianism's 'fundamental' of 'pleasure' as it is a surer guide to prevent selfishness. Alternatively, you could argue that Kantian Ethics' 'fundamental' of 'duty' is more likely to prevent atrocities than something as ambiguous and manipulable as *'agape.'* In both of these examples I have gone beyond a simple comparison of fundamentals ('X believes this, but Y believes that') to a comparative *judgement* ('X's belief in this is better than Y's belief in that because…').

Whether Fletcher's understanding of *agape* is really religious or whether it means nothing more than wanting the best for the person involved in a given situation

There are some clear indications that Situation Ethics has links to religion, but also some serious question marks about how deeply these religious links go, mirroring Fletcher's own ambiguity concerning religion. Both the Working Principles and Fundamental Principles reference religion. Under the former there is the principle of 'Positivism' which asks us to put faith before reason, and especially faith in the need to maximise *agape*. In the Fundamental Principles, Fletcher makes clear he thinks the ruling norm of Christian ethics is love. The term *'agape'* itself was frequently used by Jesus, such as in the two greatest commandments, to love God and your neighbour as yourself. Jesus also practised what he preached, such as putting aside laws not to work on the Sabbath to pick grain with his disciples: 'the Sabbath was made for man, not man for the Sabbath' also seems to chime with the

Working Principle of 'Personalism.' However, there are missed opportunities to ground Situation Ethics more deeply within Christianity. A move which would have anchored Situation Ethics more securely within Christianity would have been for Fletcher not only to make the structural move of basing the choice for *agape* on faith in 'Positivism,' but also that the faith which anchors *agape* most securely is not just any faith, but the Christian faith. For although he briefly mentioned that 'God is love,' it would have made sense for Fletcher to have argued that we should show others *agape* as God showed us *agape*, most profoundly through the death of Jesus on the cross, and that to appreciate this we need to posit God as love through an act of faith. This would have secured his theory more deeply, but perhaps at the expense of closing it off to non-Christians. Many Christians would only see Situation Ethics as having the superficial veneer of Christianity through the word *agape* and passing reference to Christianity. This is mainly for two reasons: i) what Situation Ethics could permit, and ii) Fletcher bypassing traditional authorities in the pursuit of his ethics. Combining both of these issues, nothing in principle is off limits in Situation Ethics so long as it is 'the most loving thing to do' (entered into through *agape* and maximising *agape*). This could easily go against the Bible ('thou shalt not murder') which is a significant source of moral authority, especially to Protestants, and also against the teachings of the Catholic Church. Concerning the latter, what Situation Ethics could allow might well go against all the Primary Precepts of Natural Moral Law. Stepping back and looking more theologically, Augustine, Calvin, and Barth would all have questioned whether human reasoning is sufficient in our sinful state to be making such profound moral judgements ourselves; Situation Ethics could be seen as a form of Pelagianism (where humans can save themselves and make right moral choices) which many Christians see as a 'heresy' (wrong belief) since it downplays the atoning death of Jesus Christ and the grace of God to enable humans to act rightly.

Whether or not the rejection of absolute rules by situation ethics makes moral decision-making entirely individualistic and subjective

In some ways Situation Ethics appears very subjective insofar as humans are making decisions about what is good, bad, right, and wrong all based on their own understanding both of the situation in question and what 'the most loving thing to do' would be. On the other hand, there are constraints on action according to Situation Ethics which would mean that Situation Ethics is not as permissively subjective as antinomian theories, which is precisely the point of the theory and is where Fletcher explicitly positions it. The first and most significant restriction is the first 'Fundamental Principle,' and that is *agape* as the absolute value which must be taken into account and then 'distributed' when put into action. If the absolute value of *agape* has to be taken into account, then individual judgement is held to account by a standard which transcends the subject: *agape*. This means that while the individual makes the decision, their decisions are right only if they conform to the absolute value of *agape*. Beyond this significant point, the guidance Fletcher provides in his theory provides further points which should steer the moral agent's decision-making, such as 'Personalism' and that the agent should will their neighbour's good, whether they like them or not. Really Situation Ethics is a form of moral relativism rather than subjectivism of the sort of a thinker such as Nietzsche.

Sample essay

Assess the view that Fletcher's understanding of *agape* is not religious at all (40 marks)

Situation Ethics is a teleological ethical theory which has an absolute value (*agape*) but is relativistic in its application of the value to concrete ethical situations. It was put forward by the American ethicist Joseph Fletcher in his 1966 book of the same name. I will be arguing that Situation Ethics has a Christian veneer but that it does not engage with Christianity deeply enough for Fletcher's understanding of *agape* to be religious.

My view, rightly, is that Fletcher's understanding of *agape* is not religious enough to be classified as Christian because Fletcher's understanding of *agape* is too permissive to guide what is meant by the 'most loving thing.' One might have to sacrifice one's own wellbeing, but the world is strange enough to allow eventualities which could be deemed the 'most loving.' Anthony O'Hear asked how could it ever possibly be right to throw babies onto bonfires? One might recoil upon hearing this, but what in Situation Ethics would prevent this from happening if it was deemed 'the most loving thing to do'? If the end justified the means, if people were at the centre of decision-making, if it is willing the neighbour's good on balance, then there according to Fletcher's theory there might be an obscure case where this awful thing could be regarded by someone as the 'most loving thing to do.' Dan Brown's novel *Inferno* involves a genius Bertrand Zobrist who unleashes a virus to decimate the population to prevent overpopulation which he thinks would destroy humanity. By killing people, he is trying to have respect for people. In the film adaptation, Tom Hanks' character, trying to stop Zobrist, says at the conclusion of the movie, "The greatest sins of human history were committed in the name of love!" Indeed, this is action- which could be permitted under Situation Ethics- is a sin against God as it is going against the sanctity of life principle. God is meant to give life and take it away, not humans, and one of the Ten Commandments is 'Do not murder.' Fletcher would have disagreed, pointing to Jesus' teachings and example. Fletcher would have been against the 'legalism' of the Ten Commandments, pointing out that another one of the Ten Commandments was 'Keep the Sabbath holy.' Jesus did not keep the Sabbath holy, healing and picking grain on the day of rest. If the Sabbath should not be kept holy, then why not murder if it is the most loving outcome for everyone involved in the situation? This notion of *agape* makes Jesus a relativist, and so we should do likewise. This view is wrong because it does not take the nuances of New Testament Ethics into account. While sometimes Jesus seemed to abrogate

Torah Law, elsewhere he intensifies it such as in the Antitheses where he takes another one of the Ten commandments—'Do not commit adultery'—and turns it from a physical act (having sex with someone who is not your spouse) to a state of mind (lusting after someone who is not your spouse). Of course, this is harder to follow than the Ten Commandments, so it is wrong to think that just because Jesus broke the Sabbath Law it means that all the laws are redundant. Indeed, Jesus said he came to fulfil the law, not destroy it. What, then, does this mean about what Jesus understood about 'love'? Jesus seemed to suggest that *agape* was about God loving human beings through sacrificing him, his only Son, to save humankind, and we, too, should be involved in costly self-sacrifice to help anybody else, which is what Jesus was doing breaking the Sabbath law to heal the man and prevent his disciples from going hungry; *agape* is here an attitude rather than a consequence. This is a far cry from the quasi-Utilitarian approach Fletcher took whereby '*agape*' seems something like 'overall benefit to the majority in a situation.'

My view, rightly, is that Fletcher's understanding of *agape* is not completely religious because it only has the structure of faith, not the content. This is because although Fletcher says we should 'posit' *agape* in one of his working principles, he does not ground *agape* in anything larger apart from a brief mention that 'God is love'. If he had said that we should posit *agape* because God is love because Jesus died on the cross this would have been more strongly Christian; Fletcher alludes to Niebuhr's view of Jesus' death on the cross being the example of 'perfect love,' but he does not claim this view as his own. Instead, he said we should posit on faith, rather than reason, that we should be maximising *agape* (the *most* loving thing to do is implicitly supporting this idea of maximising). Fletcher said that the ruling norm of Christian ethics should be *agape* in one of his fundamental principles, seemingly indicating that his understanding of *agape* was religious, namely Christian. Indeed, Jesus does say that the 'two greatest commandments' are 'to love God and to love your neighbour as yourself,' and the word for love is '*agape*' for both commandments. Nevertheless, as mentioned above the kind of *agape* Jesus is talking about here is a self-sacrificial attitude which is all about the intention to help others, rather than an ethical system where the 'end justifies the means' (to quote one of the other fundamental principles) and a most loving consequence can come about from malicious intentions. The issue here is that what does 'most loving' mean? It seems to refer to another standard independent of the term loving to explain what 'loving' means? Is 'most loving' something like 'the net balance of pleasure minus pain'? To use the *Inferno* example from Dan Brown, this seems to be what

Zobrist had in mind. If so, we are left with something which looks like Classical Utilitarianism dressed up in religious clothing.

Although Situation Ethics has religious garb through the language of *agape*, allusions to Christian ethics, and talk of 'faith,' these allusions clothe a secular, teleological ethic underneath. With its maximising tendencies, lack of restraint- even when innocent human life is at stake- and focus on the outcome rather than the intention, Situation Ethics' understanding of *agape* is only superficially religious.

Chapter 5: Euthanasia

Euthanasia revision summary

Key terms/ideas
- Active euthanasia
- Passive euthanasia
- Voluntary euthanasia
- Involuntary euthanasia
- Non-voluntary euthanasia
- Physician-assisted suicide
- Sanctity of Life (Strong)
- Weak Sanctity of Life
- Quality of life
- Dignitas
- Consent
- Acts and omissions
- Liberal principle
- Paternalism
- Dead donor rule
- Ordinary and extraordinary means
- Eugenics
- PVS
- Palliative care
- Slippery slope
- Vitalism
- Instrumentalism
- QALYS

Key scholars
Peter Singer, Helga Kuhse, John Stuart Mill, Jonathan Glover, Pope John Paul II, James Rachels, John Hardwig

Key quotes
'there is no evidence that [legalised euthanasia] has sent Dutch society down a slippery slope' (Helga Kuhse)
'Image of God' (Genesis)
'You shall not murder' (Exodus)
'Love is patient' (1 Corinthians)
'the Lord gave, and the Lord has taken away' (Job)
Calls for euthanasia are part of a 'conspiracy against life' (Pope JPII, *Evangelium Vitae*)

Key case studies
Reg Crew, Diane Pretty, Jack Kevorkian, Baroness Campbell, Tony Bland, Baby Charlotte, Dr David Moor

Possible questions
'Natural Law is superior to situation ethics in its treatment of issues surrounding euthanasia.' Discuss (40 marks)
'Natural law succeeds because it takes human nature seriously.' Discuss (40 marks)
'Autonomy as an ideal is unrealistic. No-one is perfectly autonomous.' Discuss with reference to the ethical issue of euthanasia. (40 marks)

'Sanctity of human life is the core principle of euthanasia.' Discuss (40 marks)

'There is no moral difference between actively ending a life by euthanasia and omitting to treat the patient.' Discuss (40 marks)

Curriculum links
- NML
- Utilitarianism
- Kant
- Situation Ethics
- Christian Moral Principles
- Problem of Evil (theodicies, Job)

Further reading
https://www.utilitarian.net/singer/by/1993----.htm
https://www.lrb.co.uk/v04/n04/jonathan-glover/letting-people-die
https://www.carenotkilling.org.uk/

Euthanasia- a brief summary

Euthanasia means 'dying well.' It usually refers to the ending of the life of someone who is terminally ill or suffering in great pain or discomfort with a serious illness. It is illegal in most countries in the world, but it is legal in a handful of countries. Switzerland is one of only places where non-nationals can go to a clinic- in this case, Dignitas- for euthanasia. Most professional organisations are against euthanasia, although it is important to note that in September 2021 the BMA moved to a 'neutral' stance on the matter. There are different kinds of euthanasia. Active euthanasia involves taking active steps to end someone's life, such as giving someone a pill or an injection. Passive euthanasia is withdrawing of treatment essential to keep someone alive. Voluntary euthanasia is where someone consents to euthanasia, involuntary where they expressly do not want it and it happens anyway (essentially murder), while non-voluntary is where euthanasia takes place where someone cannot consent (such as when they are in a PVS). No-one advocates for involuntary euthanasia; it is with voluntary and non-voluntary forms of euthanasia where there is ethical debate.

Keeping the legal issues to one side (as this is an ethics course), arguably the largest areas of debate are the sanctity of life vs quality of life debate, 'killing' vs 'letting die,' the questions of 'autonomy' and whether it can truly take place when there are pressures on people, and when euthanasia should be allowed. While these issues could be covered in the summary, the way OCR have outlined the 'issues arising from euthanasia' it makes sense to cover them there.

Issues arising from euthanasia

The application of natural law and situation ethics to euthanasia

Natural Moral Law would see euthanasia as an apparent good, not a real one. A real good would be acting on a secondary precept to avoid euthanasia, for this would be pursuing the primary precepts of 'defending the innocent' and 'order in society' by refraining from taking life, no-matter the quality of the life in question. NML's insistence on preserving innocent life is one manifestation of the 'Strong Sanctity of Life Principle.' This safeguards life insofar as it prevents a 'slippery slope' where quality-of-life value judgements are made about certain people, leading to ever-lower thresholds by which those who are not considered as valuable are allowed to be euthanised, even against their will. Spectres of Nazi euthanasia programmes have added weight to the slippery slope argument, although Helga Kuhse has pointed out these nightmares have not come to pass where euthanasia has been legalised in recent decades in places such as Holland and Switzerland. You could also point to the 'education' primary precept here as euthanasia shortens a person's life, denying them the opportunity to reflect on their life knowing death is near which can allow for spiritual growth (links can be made to Irenaeus and Hick here).

Situation Ethics would argue that NML hampers the autonomy of the person with a low quality of life. Fletcher himself campaigned for euthanasia to be made legal, and his theory of Situation Ethics explicitly puts the person at the centre of ethical decision-making rather than any legalistic considerations. If the end justifies the means and we should be willing our neighbour's good, then Fletcher thought we should be prepared to help out those who seek euthanasia if it would be the most loving thing to do, perhaps if they were suffering from a terminal, degenerative condition such as Reg Crew who was in the advanced stages of motor neurone disease in 2003 and went to Dignitas for physician-assisted suicide. While Reg Crew's case was, as Secretary General of Dignitas Ludwig A. Minelli said, 'very clear,' the problem with Situation Ethics is that it could be applied to cases which are not. What about if someone is very old and wishes to be euthanised, even if they do not have a terminal illness? Should they be allowed euthanasia? Personalism, Pragmatism, and Relativism could be dangerous here as although situations can vary and we should be putting the person at the centre of moral decision-making to do what is practical, a person could have been made to feel depressed by others around them for personal gain. Although the very old person has a consistent wish to be euthanised, they could have been made to feel like a burden. Even if others around them might well be better off if that person is no longer around in terms of time and effort spent caring for them and money for their relatives, there is a lack of justice here. Although justice is 'love distributed,' we are back with the contentious issue of what love is. Fletcher's *'agape* calculus' seems to imply that *agape* is little more than benefit, as it does not seem like a selfless attitude. If this is the case, then Fletcher's idea of justice does not seem a good one as it is unfair that this very old person should be made to feel like a burden, and other theories such as NML and Kantian Ethics have set up moral principles to protect and safeguard against exploitation of this kind. On a Kantian or NML view, palliative care would be the appropriate response to someone whose quality of life was extremely poor and their condition terminal, and this would show *agape* as a selfless attitude in Jesus' sense of the term rather than *agape* as some benefit to maximise in a teleological ethical sense.

Whether or not a person should or can have complete autonomy over their own life and decisions made about it

From a Kantian perspective, it is possible for people to have complete autonomy over their decisions as the 'noumenal' self is hived-off from the phenomenal self. In other words, we can act from a rational perspective if we so choose, ignoring our emotions. This means for Kant that it is our duty not to use ourselves solely as a means to the end of eliminating suffering, for wanting to eliminate suffering comes from a position of desire or feeling like you need to be free from pain. As such, Kant thought we could not universalise taking one's own life either ourselves or with the support of others (he may well have been reacting against Hume here again, too). Kant thought that although we should have autonomy over our own life, this autonomy does not equate to anything like libertarian freedom to choose to do whatever we want with it. Someone like Camus or Sartre may well argue that this kind of autonomy is not real autonomy as you are still be constrained by something, namely the moral law. However, the ingenious nature of Kant's ethics is that he argued that the moral is not something imposed on you from without, but something the rational will legislates for itself. Of course, the likes of Nietzsche, Marx, and Freud (and theologians such as Augustine, Calvin, and Barth) would have questioned whether we are rational in the way Kant argued we were. If we do not have a noumenal self capable of pure practical reasoning, then his argument falls down.

Most Christians would argue that humans cannot, and should not, have complete autonomy over their own life and decisions made about it. St. Paul wrote 'You are not your own,' and this flies in the face of modern liberal thinking as put forward by the likes of Mill with his 'Liberty Principle' who would have argued that humans are free to make choices about their life unless they harm other people (physically). Paul, like many Christians subsequently, thought we have our lives on loan from God, that we are stewards of the life God has allowed us to have by creating us in his image. Therefore, we should take care of ourselves as our bodies are 'temples of the Holy Spirit.' These Pauline ideas are bound-up with what is often referred to as the 'Strong Sanctity of Life Principle,' which prohibits euthanasia in all circumstances. Euthanasia would be 'playing God' and going against commandment against murder. Followers of NML would reason along similar lines, arguing that even if humans have control over their lives that they are accountable to a higher purpose given to them by God to defend their own innocent lives, and so refrain from euthanasia, which would be considered an 'apparent good,' not a 'real good.' A further, more elaborate, argument could be along the lines of predestination or determinism, that although humans feel free, they are acting in accordance with antecedent causes. Should this determinism be scientific along the lines of physical causes and effects, then this would not have such serious theological implications as predestination from God, for then people seeking euthanasia would somehow be acting in accordance with God's will despite him being against murdering according to the Ten Commandments.

Whether or not the religious concept of sanctity of life has any meaning in twenty-first century medical ethics

The concept of the sanctity of life has meaning in the twenty-first century to many religious people. A large proportion of Christians still believe that God gives life and God takes it away, prohibiting practices such as euthanasia and abortion. However, as medical technology advances, this notion of 'playing God' cuts both ways. Are doctors not playing God by prescribing life-enhancing drugs or performing life-saving surgery, for if someone was on death's door then it could be argued that it was 'their time' and God was taking their life away? If one argues that God is 'working through' doctors to save life through drugs and surgery, then the argument could be that God is working through organisations such as Dignitas to take someone's life. If it is argued that God would not wish for innocent life to be taken by other human beings due to commands such as 'Do not murder' and natural law such as 'Defend the innocent,' then by the same cherry-picking process one could point to other quotations such as 'Be merciful as your heavenly father is merciful' and 'I demand mercy, not sacrifice' in favour of euthanising people who are requesting such mercy killing. Furthermore, as is often shown in the Bible, God's plan is ultimately inscrutable, with him working in mysterious ways, which is one of the messages from the book of Job and -arguably- from the story of Abraham and Isaac, so it would be presumptuous for us to know that God does not want us to assist people who request to die. Here perhaps the 'Weak Sanctity of Life Principle' has more relevance to the twenty-first century, where life should be a gift, not a burden. Here the language moves from life being on 'loan' from God ('You are not your own') to it being a gift. If it is a gift, it should be up to humans what they do with it once the gift has been appreciated and used. With Kierkegaard's reading of the story of Abraham and Isaac, he referred to the 'teleological suspension of the ethical,' for in this instance God commanded the death of an innocent person (Isaac), although he then reversed his command. If God can command the death of an innocent person by suspending moral rules for a goal, then could this also not be the case regarding euthanasia? For the goal of relief from unbearable pain, might not God command people to seek euthanasia?

Of course, for many people in the twenty-first century, religious ideas have no meaning at all. In an interview with ITV in 2003, Ludwig A. Minelli- the Secretary General of Dignitas- looked puzzled to be asked whether he was 'playing God.' His reply was brief and dismissive: "I do not comment on religious ideas." He added that it was the ill, suffering human being themselves who should make the choice whether to seek euthanasia. Although the secularisation thesis has been debated in recent years (especially when considering Christian vs non-Christian religions), there has been a marked decline in the Christian faith in many Western European countries. Rowan Williams even went so far to refer to the United Kingdom as a 'post-Christian country.' As such, the relevance of the sanctity of life principle in medical ethical matters has become reduced, with more emphasis on the quality-of-life principle. Indeed, the latter has had institutional importance already with the QALYS measure having been used by the NHS. The large influence of liberalism in the UK over the last two hundred years has meant that people are accustomed to having choice over almost every area of their life which affects their quality of life so long as they do not harm other people (Mill's 'Liberty Principle'), and many people think that euthanasia only harms themselves meaning that there have been repeated (failed) attempts to change the law in the UK against euthanasia. Ethicists such as Peter Singer have said that one of his five 'quality of life commandments' is to acknowledge that the worth of human life varies, which flies in the face of the sanctity of life principle. How you measure 'quality of life' is difficult, however, and some take it in terms of having a basis in happiness (Bentham), autonomy (Mill), or consciousness (Glover). There are problems with all these ideas. Happiness is subjective and it is hard to know when you are happy (look for people clapping their hands). Autonomy is restricted by law, feelings, the media, our body and so much more (even the moral Law, Kant would argue). As for consciousness, does this mean we can euthanise sleeping people? This seems absurd. Less frivolously, what about people who might come out of a coma?

Whether or not there is a moral difference between medical intervention to end a patient's life and medical non-intervention to end a patient's life

In one sense there is no moral difference between medical intervention to end a patient's life and medical non-intervention to end a patient's life as the end result is the same: the person is no longer alive. For teleological theories such as Utilitarianism and Situation Ethics, this would be the salient factor. For a deontological theory such as Kant's, there is a significant difference as following the rule matters, not the consequence. As Kantian Ethics cannot sanction murder, euthanasia, or assisted suicide, it could not permit or encourage medical intervention to end a patient's life. However, if a patient died from medical non-intervention, then this could be permitted under a maxim such as 'Withhold treatment which would be extraordinary means.' The concept of 'extraordinary means,' refers to treatment where there is almost no chance of success or where there is excessive risk. This approach would also be palatable to thinkers within the Catholic tradition. For instance, adherents of NML would not be able to sanction medical intervention to end a patient's life as this would go against the primary precept to 'defend innocent life.' However, medical non-intervention to end a patient's life could be permitted under the notion of extraordinary means which amounts to passive euthanasia. It is sometimes said that the doctrine of double effect can be used from an NML perspective to justify taking steps to end a person's life, therefore in this case making ending a life and withholding treatment morally equivalent on NML grounds. For example, to sedate someone to a point where they are comfortable a doctor might end give a patient enough sedative which kills them. Their intention was to sedate the patient to make them comfortable, but the secondary effect would be to kill them. This would not be permitted under the doctrine of double effect as the intended effect (making someone comfortable) is out of proportion to the magnitude of the secondary, unintended effect of killing the person. Therefore, on NML grounds even when invoking the doctrine of double effect there is a moral difference between medical intervention to end a patient's life and medical non-intervention to end a patient's life.

Sample essay

'Situation Ethics is the best approach to issues arising from Euthanasia.' Discuss. (40)

Situation Ethics is a teleological normative ethical theory which takes *agape* (an absolute value) and relativises when making more decisions. For Joseph Fletcher, the founder of Situation Ethics in the 1960s, the right action is one done out of the intention of selfless love, to create the most loving outcome for all involved in a situation. Euthanasia is mercy killing, a 'good death,' often for those in considerable pain suffering from a terminal illness. I will be arguing that Situation Ethics is not the best approach to issues arising from euthanasia as it is too unclear and that it does not take into consideration that life is a gift from God.

My view, rightly, is that Situation Ethics is too unclear to be the best approach to issues arising from euthanasia. To avoid a slippery slope, you need clear-cut rules. By definition, Situation Ethics is against the 'legalism' of clear-cut rules, even if it is also against the 'antinomianism' of all-out moral anarchy. As Dan Brown wrote in his book *Inferno*, "The greatest sins of human history were committed in the name of love." With its working principles of 'pragmatism' and 'relativism,' an apparently well-meaning relative doctor could convince a suffering person that the most 'loving thing to do' could be to end their life, which would appear to be 'voluntary euthanasia.' On a larger scale, politicians might apply these same principles to convince whole populations that euthanising the vulnerable might be the 'most loving thing to do,' and where the is no clear line in the sand, this would be easy to do, and as Professor John Haldane and others have argued, the more it is done, the lower the threshold for involuntary and non-voluntary euthanasia becomes. Fletcher might well have unconvincingly responded that Situation Ethics has theoretical resources to prevent a slippery slope, especially the working principle 'Personalism' and the fundamental principle 'Love wills the neighbour's good.' If you care about persons as persons, and if you will their good, then this should prevent doing them harm, especially killing them. However, this response is unconvincing due to the very vagueness at the heart of Situation Ethics. What does your 'neighbour's good' mean? Who decides what is 'good' and what standard is being held up here? At least with Bentham's Classical Utilitarianism it was clear that 'good' meant 'pleasure,' and with Natural Moral Law 'good' means fulfilling a purpose given to humans by God. To say that 'good' means '*agape*' would start to become tautological, that the most loving thing to do would be to create the most loving outcome. Unfortunately, there would be some people who genuinely believe they would be doing a favour (or 'willing their neighbour's good') by killing them, whether this be with benign intentions as with a human sending their animal to a vet to be put down, or with more malevolent intentions. On the latter score, Situation Ethics is again too vague as are we meant to judge ethical rightness or wrongness by expressed intentions or by 'true' ones, only known to the person performing the action? Again, this makes Situation Ethics inadequate to deal with issues arising from euthanasia.

My view, rightly, is that Situation Ethics is not the best approach to issues arising from euthanasia as it does not uphold the view that life is a gift from God as we are made in his image with intrinsic, absolute value. The Strong Sanctity of Life Principle gives value to human life which Situation Ethics does not take seriously enough, endangering vulnerable people who could be exploited if it euthanising them is considered the most 'loving thing to do.' A strong sanctity of life approach holds legalistic rules which prevent euthanasia taking place, which goes against the fundamental principle of Situation Ethics 'Love is acted out situationally not prescriptively.' Situation Ethics' working principle of 'Relativism' and fundamental principle that 'Love is the only absolute' means that moral absolutes such as the sanctity of life principle are irrelevant for a situational approach to moral decision-making. Fletcher would admit this but see his relativism as a strength of his approach, rather than a weakness. The relativism of abandoning the sanctity of life approach gives him more flexibility than other normative ethical theories, such as Natural Moral Law, which are tied to religious ideas to do with life being sacred, as expressed in the primary precept 'Defend the innocent' which would give rise to the secondary precept to be applied in end-of-life situations, 'Do not euthanise.' Although there is some flexibility built into NML such as the 'doctrine of double effect' and the secondary precepts themselves, the flexibility extends to other issues such as abortion and war, but not to euthanasia where it is clear that ending a life for reasons of avoiding pain and discomfort are 'apparent goods' rather than 'real ones' as they frustrate the purpose of 'Defending the innocent.' By contrast, Situation Ethics' flexibility can allow for patient autonomy to consent to euthanasia if they are in pain, and this modern, largely secular ethic (albeit one related to Jesus' idea of *agape*) is more in tune with modern ideas of 'my body, my choice' than the strong sanctity of life principle of NML. The sanctity of life argument is more convincing than Fletcher's approach because it safeguards humans from exploitation, for flexibility can work against humans, especially if they become confused over their best interests. For instance, vulnerable, ill people have expressed in UK polls that they feel coerced into giving consent to euthanasia as they feel a burden. As a result, some might convince themselves that it is in the good not only of them but also of other people around them, that they should go to Dignitas for assisted suicide. For every case like Reg Crew who seemed clear-minded that he wished to end his life because of his poor quality, there are many more people who might not want to feel a 'burden' to others. While Situation Ethics' 'Personalism' is a working principle meaning people should be at the centre of ethical decision-making, not principles and laws, it does not mean that the patient's good has to be at the centre; the 'people' at the centre of a decision made situationally could be those who benefit most from a decision for euthanasia, such as a coercive family who no longer want to administer care and who perhaps are seeking an early inheritance. By contrast, the sanctity of life principle would put a clear, legalistic line in the sand against all forms of abuse and coercion of this type.

To conclude, Situation Ethics is not the best approach to issues arising from euthanasia. In fact, it is a very limited one because it is too vague and that it does not take the sanctity of life principle seriously. Both these weaknesses result in the most vulnerable people lacking the safeguards in place to prevent them from being euthanised. If it is not clear what 'good' means, then sophisticated arguments could easily be made to sound like it could be a 'good' thing for a person to be euthanised. If life has no intrinsic value, then it is easy for vulnerable people to be coerced or convinced into thinking that they are no longer of worth and that others in the situation, such as family members, would be better off if they were no longer around. As a result, a theory like NML would be more appropriate to deal with issues arising from euthanasia as it is clearer and has the sanctity of life at its core.

Chapter 6: Business Ethics

Business Ethics revision summary

Key terms/ideas
- Corporate social responsibility
- Stakeholder
- Human dignity
- Usury
- Common good
- Solidarity
- Subsidiarity
- Fraternity
- Reciprocity
- Sustainability
- Free market economy
- Whistle-blowing
- Globalisation
- Employer
- Employee
- Stockholder
- Exploitation
- Consumer
- Business

Key scholars
Milton Friedman, Robert C. Solomon, Cardinal Vincent Nichols, Peter Singer, John Stuart Mill, Kant, Adam Smith, Karl Marx

Key documents
A Blueprint for Better Business
Mater et Magister
Equal Pay Act

Key quotes
'The business of business is business' (Milton Friedman)
'The love of money is the root of all evil' (1 Timothy 6:10)

Key case studies
- Enron
- Volkswagen
- Primark
- Nike
- Amazon
- Sports Direct
- Banc de Binary
- Cadburys
- Erin Brokovich
- Jose Bove

Possible questions

'Kantian Ethics is a better approach than Utilitarianism when it comes to issues arising from Business Ethics' – discuss (40 marks)

'The concept of corporate social responsibility is nothing more than 'hypocritical window-dressing' covering the greed of a business intent on making profits'- discuss (40 marks)

'Human beings can flourish in the context of capitalism and consumerism'- discuss (40 marks)

'Globalisation discourages the pursuit of good ethics as the foundation of good business' – discuss (40 marks)

Curriculum links
- NML
- Utilitarianism
- Kant
- Situation Ethics
- Christian Moral Principles
- Marx

Further reading

https://plato.stanford.edu/entries/ethics-business/

https://peped.org/philosophicalinvestigations/ethics/ethics-a2/business-ethics/

Business Ethics: a brief summary

Business Ethics has been something of a growth area of the past fifty years. The 'ethical dollar' has become an important one, with an increasing number of companies flaunting their ethical credentials in statements of corporate social responsibility, particularly in recent years regarding how 'green' a company is, leading the cynical to wonder for what purpose. For some companies their ethics seem to be central to their identity, such as the cosmetics retailer, Lush, who have been consistently against animal cruelty. Other companies have evolved over time, sometimes in the face of criticisms concerning previous practices, to be leaders in matters ethical, such as McDonalds. Central to the complexity of Business Ethics is the question about what should take priority: what is a business about? Is it about making money first and foremost? Or is it about providing a service to the community first and foremost? Or is it a corporate agent which has the same moral responsibility to others as a body of people as possessed by an individual moral agent? If, as many people suggest, 'The business of business is business' (Milton Friedman), then is this main aim an overriding aim? In other words, should the pursuit of its principal aim be pursued at all costs, or are there limits? By contrast, Robert Solomon argued that 'The purpose of business is to provide the 'things that make ordinary life easier'.' One can think of the washing machine as an example of a domestic appliance supplied by businesses in that line of retail which has made the lives of average people better, saving them time to spend on other things. As such, Solomon saw businesses as not existing in isolation but connected to other areas of life in such a way that they should not be pursuing the bottom line at all costs. Solomon thought that as businesses were connected in so many ways that it is essential for them to conduct themselves ethically, gaining trust, respect and keeping promises, for instance. To do this, Solomon developed business ethics within an Aristotelian framework, keeping virtues in mind, looking for balance in order for both the businesses themselves, as well as individuals and communities within and without the business to flourish. Cardinal Vincent Nichols added a religious dimension to the notion that businesses are about more than profit in his 'Blueprint for Better Business,' which contains five principles of a purpose-driven business, such as being a good citizen, being honest and fair with customers and suppliers. Sometimes the distinction between Friedman and Solomon/Nichols is known as the difference between the stockholder and stakeholder approaches.

Two, connected factors pertaining to businesses lend themselves to difficult ethical issues. One is the imbalance of power relations within stakeholders. The second is the globalised world in which businesses operate. For the most part, companies are hierarchical, from owners and directors all the way down to entry level and casual workers. Typically, the further up the company one goes, the betters the terms and conditions, as well as the greater the power. Abuse of power is tempting, and some companies have developed cultures which have normalised, or even encouraged and incentivised, abuse of power, such as the failed American energy giant, Enron which collapsed in 2001. Abuse of power is magnified in a globalised world by large multinational corporations using cheap labour from LEDCs, although this is not without a negative effect on less skilled workers in MEDCs for their job opportunities are reduced when labour is outsourced, even if they are beneficiaries of cheaper goods and services. Issues of justice arise, then, within companies and between companies and their suppliers.

There are more niche areas regarding corporate wrongdoing from which ethical issues arise, too, such as espionage and whistleblowing. Espionage involves everything from spying to sabotage and it is more widespread than commonly recognised. Spying has been traditionally associated with governments, but it has long been a feature of business disputes, too. I have heard first-hand from PR companies about 'spoiler campaigns.' One such PR company arranged for journalists to be flown to Las Vegas when a rival of the telecommunications company for whom they had a contract was launching a new phone to reduce the amount of press coverage the competitor would acquire for the new release. The obvious ethical question concerns whether this is right to do or not, but there is a less obvious- but no less important- ethical question about how a business should respond when they find out they are on the receiving end of espionage. During the Cold War there was frequently technological espionage. I have heard a story that one side realised they were being spied on by another side, with cutting edge plane designs being stolen. When they found out, the side being stolen from did not let on they knew, leaving out subtly faulty designs. These subtle faults were not picked up on, being incorporated into the final design leading to a fatal plane crash. Whistleblowing might be exposing espionage or another kind of wrongdoing, such as 'creative' accounting, exploitation of workers, or damaging the environment. It involves telling a superior within the company about wrongdoing, giving management a chance to right the wrong before an external organisation or individual shines a light on whatever is being done wrong and punishes the organisation (or at least some people within it). Sherron Watkins was a whistle-blower at Enron in a case of extremely creative accounting among other irregularities.

Issues arising from Business Ethics

The application of Kantian ethics and utilitarianism to business ethics

Kantian Ethics has an interesting approach to Business Ethics. Kant famously put forward his 'shopkeeper' example to illustrate his ethics. An honest shopkeeper is doing the right thing, but is he doing so for the right reasons? If he is charging an honest price to entice customers, Kant would argue he is not acting morally for he is working on the basis of the maxim, 'If you want custom, charge an honest price,' which is a hypothetical imperative and is based on emotions, such as desiring custom. If the shopkeeper did the same thing but for nothing other than the reason of doing his duty of being honest, then this would be acting according to the Categorical Imperative and so would be the morally right thing to do for the right reasons. While the idea of being honest for its own sake is endearing and noble, I am not convinced it conforms to the reality of running a business. Milton Friedman would agree with me here for he was a business realist, with the purpose of business to make a profit. Kant's issue with this would be what if achieving more custom entailed being dishonest? This would be going against the Categorical Imperative. To resolve this issue, it is perhaps worth looking more deeply into whether the Categorical Imperative can work at all in a business setting. While the issue of consistency in being honest has meant I have focused so far on the first formulation, the second formulation reveals the weaknesses of applying Kantian Ethics to issues in Business Ethics. While the second formulation works well in sexual ethical issues such as sexual assault as this is clearly using someone solely as a means to an end of your own gratification, it does not work so well in Business Ethics. When you are hailing a taxi, are you using the taxi driver solely as a means to an end? You pay him fairly, but you are only interested in getting to the airport promptly. You are not interested in him as a person, even though you are not discourteous, let alone hostile or unfair, to him. The sheer number of interactions with people- in person and online- to do with business, especially retail business, means that you are almost certainly having to treat some of these people solely as a means to an end. The specific issue is identifying the distinction between what it means to treat someone as a means to an end (which is not a problem) and solely as a means to an end (which is).

My gut feeling would be that most businesses work on something related to a Utilitarian basis, albeit with a bias towards their own pleasure or preferences. An example of doing so would be the (in)famous Ford Pinto case from the 1970s. Early on in the car's lifetime it was found there was a problem the gas tank. To recall the car would have cost a little amount of money to a lot of customers, while keeping the car as it was would have cost a lot of money to few people (namely Ford) in paying compensation to people (or their families) injured or killed in explosions caused by rear end collisions with the Pinto. Using actuarial calculations concerning burns, deaths, and the number of likely incidents, Ford worked out that less suffering would be caused by letting the car go out with the design flaw than recalling it. Using this monetised form of Negative Utilitarianism (where the emphasis is on reducing suffering rather than maximising happiness), Ford found a way of reducing the money spent on this potential recall issue. The final figures justified their approach if you accept their premises. One issue with their premises is that they equated 'losing money' with 'suffering.' Another issue was them putting a price on human life, although they were accepting the problematic actuarial measure from the time. Of course, a sanctity of life approach held by many religions would have a problem with this approach. It does allow humans to be used solely as a means to an end here, something which Kant would have been against. Therefore, both NML and Kantians would disagree with the Utilitarian approach on deontological grounds pertaining to the devaluing human life. There is also the justice issue of using a Utilitarian approach of abusing those in the minority. If the majority – the business, consumers, stockholders—would be happier if a relatively small number of workers in an LEDC produced goods in a sweatshop, this would justify these workers being paid an unfair amount, something most people would regard as problematic, although on what grounds depends on your ethical theory.

Whether or not the concept of corporate social responsibility is nothing more than 'hypocritical window-dressing' covering the greed of a business intent on making profits

Some businesses will be trying to disguise their greed with statements of corporate social responsibility in order to sell their goods and services to green-minded consumers who are taken-in by such statements. It is quite easy to use the internet to search for business scandals—especially to do with the environment—and see them at odds with the rhetoric on the same business' website. In defence of these companies, it could be argued that these scandals are in the past and the websites are reflecting the company's newfound wish to move on and show the ways in which they have learned from their mistakes. It could also be argued that, especially in large multinational corporations, scandals might well have been caused by rogue employees. Hypocrisy is easier to pin on individual moral agents than corporations made up of many individuals, all with their own wills, values, and actions. There is a link here to made to 'Realism' in the context of war ethics, where governments are allowed to do things that individuals cannot because they have greater responsibility. Interestingly, Niebuhr's 'Christian Realism' says that this is inevitable in a fallen world. Away from businesses who are simply using statements of corporate social responsibility to chase the 'green dollar,' there will be other sincere businesses who are not using such statements as window dressing. This view would only not hold if any and every business held Friedman's view that 'the business of business is business,' but given the variety of human motivations it is unlikely every business owner purporting to care about ethics is lying in order to gain more custom.

Whether or not human beings can flourish in the context of capitalism and consumerism

Capitalism refers to the system of government which permits private ownership. Consumerism is a society based around consumption of goods and services in order to fuel the economy. As for flourishing, this is understood variously but has strong Aristotelian connotations and implies humans have a *telos*. In favour of the idea of humans being able to flourish, in theory in a consumer-capitalist system everyone can work up and do better if they are go-getters and other people can receive more if the go-getters are allowed to prosper. This is Reaganism, 'trickle-down economics.' In terms of 'order in society' which is part of what Aquinas thought it meant for people to flourish, everyone is treated the same insofar as you are all consumers. Stephen Pinker's *Enlightenment Now* makes a strong case for humans flourishing in health, free time, money, standards of living, education (such as literacy rates) and self-reported levels of wellbeing in a consumer-capitalist system. What is the alternative? Communism? This might work in theory but to what extent does it work in practice? Pinker makes the case that where societies are closed and tightly regulated by governments, people flourish less against the above-mentioned measures of flourishing. These measures chime well with NML: standards of living and health link to 'ordered society' and 'defend the innocent' in terms of primary precepts, while literacy rates and education refer to the primary precept of 'education.' Capitalist societies also experience population booms, which links to 'reproduction.' The only dubious one is 'worship God' as many of these consumer-capitalist societies (with a notable exception of the USA) often become secularised. Jesus was said to have exclaimed that 'You cannot serve two masters: God and money.' It is not hard to see consumer-capitalist societies as money-worshipping, with shopping centres replacing cathedrals and consumption replacing worship. As such, Thomists would see consumer-capitalist societies as not allowing humans to flourish fully as human beings. Away from NML, consumer-capitalist societies promote greed and over-consumption, going against the Aristotelian understanding of virtue in Book 1 of his Ethics which talks about *eudaimonia* coming from a life lived in balance. Planned obsolescence also means goods wear out, requiring humans to keep working and keeping money streams coming in to allow them to afford to replace their goods.

Whether globalisation encourages or discourages the pursuit of good ethics as the foundation of good business

On a Kantian Ethics basis, globalisation discourages the pursuit of good ethics as the foundation of good business as it makes exploitation easier, and so those tempted to be greedy will have more opportunity to exercise their greed, therefore acting from emotion rather than reason (and hence not morally). That the producers of goods and services in LEDCs are remote to the consumers makes it easier for the consumers to exploit them, too, as they are not seen; as Hume recognised, it is easier to act morally to people known to us than unknown. However, another aspect of globalisation is that information and communications technologies are making the world 'shrink,' allowing humans to know almost instantly about abuses happening around the world, allowing consumers to learn about where their goods and services are coming from, enabling them to use platforms such as Twitter to hold businesses to account by publicly 'shaming' them. As such, globalisation could be seen to encourage the pursuit of good ethics as the foundation of good business as companies are increasingly realising they will be caught out through social media in particular. Whether companies are changing their practices out of fear of being exposed or from the genuine development of a conscience is another matter, and Kant would say that the former would not be genuinely ethical as per his 'shopkeeper' example. On Utilitarian grounds, it could be argued that globalisation allows for the greatest happiness of the greatest number even when exploitation occurs as consumers in MEDCs get cheaper, plentiful goods, business owners record greater profits, and even the workers in LEDCs have some jobs (and therefore money) than none (or few) at all. Kant would disagree with this as it is still treating these workers solely as a mean to an end, and so any maxim based on exploitation could not be rationally universalised.

Sample essay

'Kantian Ethics is a better approach than Utilitarianism when it comes to issues arising from Business Ethics:' Discuss (40 marks)

Kantian Ethics is a deontological, absolutist approach to ethics based on reason. By contrast, Utilitarianism is a relativistic, teleological theory which uses reason to make ethical judgements. Issues arising from Business Ethics include globalisation, whistleblowing, and the treatment of employees. I will argue that Kantian Ethics provides the best approach to issues arising from Business Ethics.

Kantian Ethics is a better approach to issues arising from Business Ethics because it safeguards minorities from exploitation, unlike Utilitarianism. This benefit becomes evident when considering the issues of globalisation and treatment of employees arising from Business Ethics. In an inter-connected world, transnational corporations such as Nike might find it tempting to take a stockholder approach to running a business, outsourcing the production of goods to developing countries where they can maximise profit by paying low wages, exploiting workers who often must labour (and live) in poor conditions. Kant would have regarded this practice as treating someone merely as a means to an end, according to his second formulation of the Categorical Imperative. As such, exploiting employees is not treating someone with the respect they deserve as rational, autonomous self-legislators, so such treatment could not be universalised. By contrast, Utilitarians would have fewer reservations about treating an employee this way so long as it were in the greatest happiness of the greatest number of people. Measured quantitatively, Bentham might have wrongly thought that paying the workers in a developing country less would have contributed to a greater 'extent' of happiness as not only would these workers be paid rather than starve, but also the Nike shareholders' profits would increase and consumers in developing countries would have to pay less for goods than if they were manufactured in MEDCs. The 'intensity' of pleasure coming to the shareholders might also be factored in here, as well as the 'fecundity' in the business receiving enough profits to continue operating and the workers in the LEDC having enough money to continue to feed themselves and their families. However, Bentham's argument is less convincing than Kant's on this issue as where does one stop calculating? If one is taking the happiness of the workers, shareholders, and consumers into account, why does it not consider the happiness of the unemployed low-skilled workers in MEDCs who have lost their jobs when transnational corporations such as Nike have relocated their factories which is not in the spirit of what Cardinal Vincent Nichols calls 'fraternity'? At least with Kant there are clearer rules about what one should do or not do given that according to the first formulation of the Categorical Imperative the moral law is 'universal,' rather than vague consequentialist guidelines which one can manipulate seemingly to justify almost anything.

Kantian Ethics is a better approach than Utilitarianism to issues arising from whistleblowing because a principled approach to running your business is not only the right thing to do, but also can prevent it from utter destruction. Kant thought that one should always be honest in business for its own sake, such as the grocer doing his duty of charging the right price simply for its own sake, regardless of the consequences. This is underscored by Kant holding the 'good will' as the only intrinsic good, which 'shines forth like a precious jewel,' which means doing duty for duty's sake. Whistleblowing involves doing your duty to be honest and telling the truth, even if it is not easy to do so. Sherron Watkins was brave to tell the truth to the chief executives at Enron when it became apparent that the 'creative accounting' was deeply corrupt. Some Utilitarians would think that Watkins' whistleblowing might have contributed to the toppling of the house of cards which brought down Enron, leading to the destruction of reputations and pensions. Even Preference Utilitarians such as Singer who try to be 'impartial spectators,' might have wrongly avoided blowing the whistle because they might have considered the consequences of blowing it as going against their preference to continue being paid, as well as a similar preference to all the others in the business, especially as Milton Friedman thought 'the business of business is business.' However, the Kantian position is more convincing than the Preference Utilitarian one here because its intention sets an example: to tell the truth and be honest in bringing corruption to light shows that bad practice can be called out, even at a personal cost. Enron got into this bad situation in the first place whereby the whistle had to be blown through lying and corruption, and so this gives credence to the Kantian position that telling the truth in a courageous way is a better approach. This is why Robert Solomon said 'Good ethics is good business,' for attempts to try to justify business decisions which are self-serving, even if backed up through some half-baked Utilitarian approach, can backfire spectacularly, such as in the case of Enron. The Kantian intention would not be for the business to flourish but for the truth to be told, but as a happy by-product, good ethics is good business. The Kantian approach has the further benefit over the Utilitarian one as the decision would derive from autonomous reasoning, drawing upon the free will of the 'noumenal self,' rather than a preference which might be rooted in desires and inclinations to escape punishment. Kant would argue that a desire to escape punishment is based on the phenomenal self and so is outside of control. Ultimately, who would want to run a business and make decision in a runaway, 'out of control' fashion?

In conclusion, Kantian Ethics is a better approach to issues arising from Business Ethics than Utilitarianism. Kantian Ethics provides clear, defensible rules which can be universalised, prevent exploitation of workers and bring corruption to light, setting an example to other businesses. By contrast, Utilitarianism can be manipulated to try to justify almost anything as it lacks clarity concerning where to stop calculating. Moreover, basing more decisions (such as whether or not to blow the whistle when wrongdoing is detected) on feelings (as Utilitarians would, at least in part) is out of control, compared with the cool, rational approach advocated by Kant.

Chapter 7: Conscience

Revision summary: Conscience

Key terms/ideas

Aquinas

- *Synderesis*
- *Conscientia*
- Vincible ignorance
- Invincible ignorance
- Real good
- Apparent good

Freud

- Id
- Ego
- Superego
- Neurosis
- Psychosexual development stages (oral, anal, phallic, latent, genital)

Key scholars

Aquinas, St. Paul, Butler, Newman, Augustine, Jerome Fromm, Piaget, Kohlberg, Nietzsche, Freud

Key documents

Summa Theologica,
Totem and Taboo
The Future as an Illusion

Quotes

'To disparage the dictate of reason is equivalent to condemning the command of God' (Aquinas)
'Reason in man is rather like God in the world' (Aquinas)

'the law are written on their hearts, their consciences also bearing witness' (St. Paul)

Possible questions

Critically compare Aquinas and Freud's views on conscience (40 marks)

To what extent is conscience is linked to reason? (40 marks)

How far is conscience linked to the unconscious mind? (40 marks)

'Conscience is nothing but an umbrella term covering various factors involved in moral decision-making, such as culture, environment, genetic predisposition and education'- discuss (40 marks)

Curriculum links
- NML
- Christian Moral Principles
- Situation Ethics
- Freud

Further reading

http://www.aquinasonline.com/Questions/conscience.htm
https://plato.stanford.edu/entries/conscience-medieval/

Conscience: a brief summary

A famous film contained the line: 'Always let conscience be your guide.' Should it? If so, what does it mean? Perhaps unsurprisingly, there have been many ways in which to understand conscience. The OCR specification requires you to focus on two highly contrasting ones: Aquinas' and Freud's. Aquinas' understanding of conscience essentially reduced it to the use of reason, and it dovetails with his theory of Natural Moral Law; a conscience question on Aquinas is a good opportunity to make appropriate 'synoptic links' with NML (and a Freud conscience question an opportunity to make links with the 'Challenge of Secularism' Theology topic).

Conscience has two aspects for Aquinas: *synderesis* and *conscientia*. The former is an inclination all humans have to 'do good and avoid evil,' as well as an ability to reason our way to understanding both our human nature and its implications for ethical decision-making, what in NML are referred to as 'primary precepts.' Humans having *synderesis* is because we have been made in the image of God. The other part of our conscience, *conscientia*, is the ability to apply our theoretical knowledge of the good (our understanding of our purpose) derive secondary precepts from the primary ones and to select them to apply to concrete situations in which the moral agent finds themselves. Even if following reasons sometimes leads to bad outcomes, Aquinas thought we should always follow our reason, which essentially to him meant our conscience. Faults in our reasoning do not derive from bad motivations, Aquinas though, but from ignorance, which comes in two types: invincible and vincible ignorance. We are responsible for the latter, but not the former. With invincible ignorance, we were ignorant of a factor crucial to making a good decision (one which accords with promoting human flourishing) which we could not have been expected to know. An example here might be booking a holiday for a friend as a present. The plane carrying your friend to your holiday destination goes down over the ocean, killing him and all others on board. Although your friend would not have died had you not booked the holiday for them as a present, you should not feel blame or be blamed as the plane crashed due to a mechanical failure you could not have possibly known about. Although you were ignorant of it, you- sat behind your laptop and booking a flight from a reputable company- are not an aviation engineer, you did due diligence on the plane, and you were not permitted to inspect the plane before take-off. Vincible ignorance, by contrast, is ignorance about something which you should be expected to know about and so is blameworthy. Imagine your friend had in fact made it for their holiday and their plane did not crash in the ocean. They are enjoying Australia, but perhaps a little too much. The Australian police pull them over driving erratically in their hire car. Once breathalysed, it is apparent they are well over the legal alcohol limit. Your friend's plea of ignorance is not plausible as

Australian laws are similar to British ones and also signing forms to lease the hire car required you to acknowledge that you have read the laws for driving in Australia. Of course, everyone makes mistakes (although hopefully not many people as badly as drink driving), and so Aquinas thought we could train and develop our consciences. Although we have the *synderesis* principle to 'do good and avoid evil' from birth, we are weak at reasoning early in life and so need to learn from our mistakes to develop *'phronesis,'* or 'practical wisdom,' at knowing how to apply *'conscientia'* with more skill and effectiveness. As such, Aquinas certainly did not think conscience was a God-given 'thing,' such as a set of laws or rules or a voice of God such as variously Augustine, Newman, and (arguably) St. Paul thought it was. Instead, although we 'have' an inclination to pursue goodness, we must develop an ability we have been given to reason by God to pursue the right things in life (real goods) and avoid superficial ones (apparent goods).

By contrast, Freud was sceptical about the value of reason. Along with Marx and Nietzsche, Freud did much to destroy the Enlightenment dream of the primacy of reason. Of course, Aquinas was no Enlightenment figure, but he put as much store by reason as an Enlightenment figure such as Kant. Instead, Freud thought the human individual was at the mercy of forces outside of his control. This was expressed through Freud's tripartite theory of the mind. The first part of the mind was the id, which is unconscious and contains drives such as *'eros'* and *'thanatos,'* the 'sex' and 'death' drives, respectively. The next part of the mind develops is the ego, the conscious part of the mind which contemplates decisions and presents itself to the world. The final part of the mind which develops is also unconscious, and that is the 'superego,' which in Freud's theory functions like the conscience, providing both values and feelings of guilt. The superego internalises society's mores and values through the refractory medium of the primary parental figure(s) in a child's life. How the child reacts to these external stimuli will depend upon a variety of factors, from the strength of the drives present in their id, to the strength and methods of their parental figures, to how well they negotiate the stages of psychosexual development (the oral, anal, phallic, latency, and genital); over or under stimulation at one or more of these stages lead to 'neuroses' and 'complexes' which cause everything from quirks in personality to deviance. The ego is the battleground between the id and superego and in some readings of Freud the ego has no control, for Freud on this view takes a 'mechanistic' understanding of how decisions are made solely based on unconscious factors such as the comparative strength of the id versus the superego. The most delicate complex to negotiate is the Oedipus/Electra complex which involves the child desiring the parent of the opposite sex and feeling threatened by the same sex parent. Cultural prohibitions of incest have come through the superego, which result in a conflict with the id which needs to be satisfactorily resolved in order for the child to have healthy relationships with their parents. Freud drew heavily on James Frazer's myth of the 'old man' from primeval times, found in his then-influential book *The Golden Bough*. The old man had kept the girls and women in the tribe for himself. Jealous younger beta males killed him to appropriate the females for themselves. Later they felt guilty for this and so arose a taboo concerning incest which has been passed on. The 'old man' could, if theologised, come to represent God. Indeed, Freud—following Feuerbach who said 'man created God in his own image'—thought that religion was a psychological defence-mechanism created by humans for this purpose. As such, in *The Future as an Illusion* he thought that the development of religion was stimulated with the longing for a father generated out of the Oedipus Complex. Indeed, particularly in Christianity you can see the language of 'God the Father' being something like an idealised father figure or a way to deal with guilt for the desiring your parent, a father who is kind and merciful rather than potentially vengeful. Freud's developmental approach to conscience inspired other thinkers such as Erich Fromm, Jean Piaget, and Lawrence Kohlberg.

Issues arising from Conscience

Comparison between Aquinas and Freud:
  o on the concept of guilt

Freud deals with the concept of guilt far better than Aquinas for he is interested in it as a psychological phenomenon, explaining how we acquire feelings of guilt (going against the superego), to how we deal with them (such as setting up defence mechanisms such as religious ideas about God). Aquinas was more interested in establishing responsibility. St. Paul would say it makes more sense for guilt to be going against the laws 'written on your heart,' for – to paraphrase H. P. Owen—for every command implies a commander to whom we feel guilt. Erikson would have thought that feeling guilt means children have reached a stage of moral development where we have can make decisions for ourselves and are not overdirected by adults. Augustine would have thought that guilt is something all of us inherit regardless of moral deeds as it is bound-upon with a guilt humanity shares for Adam's first sin.

  o on the presence or absence of God within the workings of the conscience and
  super-ego

God figures indirectly in the workings of the conscience for both Aquinas and Freud. For Aquinas, God provides both the capacity for rationality through creating humans and the laws for them to follow through 'natural law.' God for Freud comes to represent the idealisation of the father figure as a way for humans to deal with their incestual feelings in the Oedipus Complex, or as a version of the 'old man' in the *Totem and Taboo* narrative taken over from Frazer. Freud's theory commits the 'genetic fallacy' of reducing the truth of a concept to its origins, a technique perfected by Nietzsche in his *Genealogy of Morality*. Aquinas takes perhaps a too optimistic view of human nature in thinking humans could be as rational as he had hoped; certainly Augustine, Calvin, and Barth would have disagreed with him.

o on the process of moral decision-making

One reading of Freud is that he put forward a mechanistic view of the mind in which the process of moral decision-making is divorced from reason and is simply the battle between the comparative strength of the id and superego. By contrast, Aquinas sees a process as beginning with *synderesis*, with moral motivation and knowledge of moral principles coming from being made in God's image with an ability to reason theoretically, to thinking more concretely using *conscientia* to discern and apply secondary precepts; reflection on the latter would help moral decision-making improve through gaining *phronesis*. Freud's approach is reductionist and pessimistic, whereas Aquinas' is perhaps too optimistic.

Whether conscience is linked to, or separate from, reason and the unconscious mind

For Freud, the conscience is separate from reason and is located in the unconscious mind in the superego battling the other element of the unconscious mind: the id. That which feeds the superego is separate from reason, too, insofar as these are myths and other cultural events. Of course, Aquinas thinks that conscience is directly identifiable with reason and the process of moral reasoning. There is some indication Aquinas thought we could reason better through gaining experience, but this is linked to learning from mistakes rather than cognitive development, unlike twentieth-century cognitive or developmental psychologists such as Piaget, Erikson, and Kohlberg. While Freud was instrumental in developing the idea of children developing their mind and sense of morality, he divorced this from reasoning. Fromm- influenced by Freud- would have seen conscience as separate from reason in his 'authoritarian conscience' view of conscience as it is a conditioned response to authority figures.

Whether conscience exists at all or is instead an umbrella term covering various factors involved in moral decision-making, such as culture, environment, genetic predisposition and education

The term 'exists' implies something ontological. Very few thinkers have thought conscience was a 'thing,' such as a homunculus like Jiminy Cricket. Arguably St. Paul thought conscience 'existed' as the law of God 'written on your heart,' although his seems like poetic language. Augustine thought conscience was the voice of God. Aquinas thought conscience was a capacity for reasoning rather than anything cultural, environmental, genetic or to do with education exception in the sense of phronesis, the practical reasoning gained from reflecting on moral decision-making. Freud thought the superego was acquired through cultural and educational influences (particularly your parents' guidance). Cognitive psychologists have seen the development of conscience intertwined with childhood development, which is a mixture of genetic, cultural, educational factors. Dr Jim Fallon is living embodiment on the importance of mixing genetics and upbringing when it comes to conscience. Born with a variant of the MAOA gene (the warrior gene) and other 'risky' genetics, he had what he says was a wonderful upbringing. Although impulse and without a sense of remorse, he has ended up a professor of biology rather than behind bars. He 'knows' what is right and wrong but he says he does not feel it deeply.

Sample essay:

'There is no such thing as a conscience'- discuss (40 marks)

Conscience is widely defined as the inner sense of right and wrong that affects our behaviour or reflects upon the goodness or otherwise of our actions, providing guilt for wrongdoing and feelings of affirmation for right actions. The question of whether conscience exists ('is a thing') is a difficult one to answer, but I believe that it does, and by 'exists' I mean is innate, absolute and is distinguished from mere moral development.

In favour of the argument that there is such a thing as a conscience, St. Paul rightly says that our conscience is 'written on our heart.' In other words, this means that the law of God is given to use by him when we are born and it exists as part of our being, an idea which can be connected to God making us in his image. We feel guilt when we break these laws and even non-Christians understand what God has commands them to do, even if they do not realise that this message has come from God. Freud wrongly disagrees with St. Paul through his concept of the id. Rather than being born with moral commands and a capacity to feel guilt, Freud thought humans are born with innate drives towards sex (*eros*) and death (*Thanatos*). The id is part of the unconscious mind and what he regarded to be a conscience—the superego—is only developed later to help the ego (the conscious part of the mind) keep the id in check. For Freud there is no such 'thing' as a conscience if by 'thing' we are talking about an innate, absolute standard of morality, for any morals we do have are acquired through socialisation and can vary between societies for our parents are the primary refractory medium through which we receive our moral code and sense of guilt. St. Paul's account of the conscience is more compelling than Freud's because we can empirically verify through sociological, legal, and historical studies how the legal and moral codes of societies world-wide are remarkably similar in core, fundamental regards; a society which advocates murder or rape or theft as the norm cannot be called to mind. Although St. Paul ontologised conscience more than Aquinas who thought of conscience more as an inclination for, and a capacity of, moral reasoning, the latter would have supported St. Paul over Freud by saying that humans have an innate sense to 'do good and avoid evil' (the *synderesis* principle). As humans have never lived in a society of moral anarchy, it is more plausible to believe that humans are born with a thing called a conscience which then gets encoded as societal rules which a handful of individuals break, rather than humans being born without such a thing as a conscience who then have to become socialised with variable degrees of success.

Another argument in favour of there being such a thing as a conscience is that human beings feel guilt. Augustine would say that all human beings inherit the guilt from Adam and Even due to them having committed the first sin against God by eating the forbidden fruit. If all humans inherit this original sin, then all humans feel guilt, and if all humans feel guilt then all humans must have a conscience. However, some humans do not seem to feel guilty as they are psychopaths who feel no empathy, guilt, or remorse for the terrible things they have done. Nietzsche wrongly thought that humans could also go 'beyond good and evil' by setting up their own moral codes guilt-free and have no accountability to anyone, let alone God. However, Nietzsche's argument is less compelling, for even if biology in the form of Darwin's theory of evolution casts doubt on a literal reading of Augustine's account of the fall and the transmission of original sin as it is extremely unlikely all humans descended from Adam and Eve, biology does tell us that most humans are hard-wired to feel guilt for wrongdoing and feelings of empathy for one another, for the brain scans of psychopaths show a lack of temporal lobe activity in places such as the orbital cortex and prefrontal cortex. Psychopaths are the exception that prove the rule for they are seen to be born without the genetics needed for their brains to develop the correct feelings and intuitions which give rise to a conscience. Why God would allow such biological divergence is a mystery and is more relevant to a discussion of the problem of evil, but it is interesting that psychopaths are largely viewed as lacking something crucial for being human. Even well-socialised individuals with the genetics and brain patterns of a psychopath, such as Dr Jim Fallon, acknowledges he feels a lack of guilt for things he has done wrong, indicating that all but psychopaths are born with a sense of guilt and shame which is hard-wired into us. Although Fallon's behaviour was guided by his socialisation, his lack of senses of guilt and empathy were part of his biological make-up.

Although Freud thought that humans are not born with a conscience and Nietzsche thought that feelings of guilt can, and should, be transcended by *Ubermenschen*, they are wrong. St. Paul thought, ontologically and nomologically, the law of God is written on the heart of all humans at birth, evidence for which comes from the lack of moral anarchy we have witnessed across societies since the dawn of civilisation. Even if one jettisons the ontological dimension of conscience, Aquinas thought humans are born with a rational inclination to do good and avoid evil, rather than to seek sex and death as Freud thought; it would take more than good socialisation to stifle this instinct, and empirical studies (sociology, criminology, history) show that law-breaking is the exception, not the rule. Finally, our sense of guilt seems to be normative. Although Augustine attributed universal guilt to a Fall of epic proportions originating from a literal Adam and Eve, the study of psychopaths has shown there is a biological basis for our inclination to care for others (empathy) and feel shame for when we have broken moral laws (guilt), for psychopaths are the exception which proves the rule that there is such a thing as a conscience, and it is very much hard-wired into humans.

Chapter 8: Metaethics

Metaethics revision summary

Key terms/ideas
- Hume's fork
- Analytic
- Synthetic
- Cognitivism
- Non-cognitivism
- Realism
- Anti-realism
- Naturalism
- Intuitionism
- Error Theory
- Divine Command Theory
- Ideal Observer Theory
- Subjectivism
- Objectivism
- Logical Positivism
- Emotivism
- Prescriptivism

Key scholars
F. H. Bradley, G. E. Moore, W. D. Ross, H. A. Prichard, A. J. Ayer, C. L. Stevenson, R. M. Hare, J. L. Mackie, Bernard Williams

Key quotes
'Good is good, and that is the end of the matter.' (G. E. Moore)

'The word intuition so used, has nothing to do with the idea of an inexplicable hunch. It simply means understanding.' (D. D. Raphael)

'The word intuition is always a signal that something has gone badly wrong.' (MacIntrrye)

'You cannot reduce morality to a set of cheers and boos.' (Mel Thompson)

Possible questions

To what extent should the meaning of the word 'good' be the defining question in the study of ethics? (40 marks)

To what extent can people just know within themselves what is good, bad, right and wrong through a 'common sense approach' to ethics? (40 marks)

To what extent are ethical terms such as good, bad, right and wrong objective? If they're not objective, what are they? (40 marks)

To what extent are ethical terms meaningful? (40 marks)

Curriculum links
- NML
- Utilitarianism
- Kantian Ethics

Further reading

https://www.iep.utm.edu/metaethi/

Good clear summary with some helpful strengths and weaknesses

http://jakedoesrevision.blogspot.com/2013/01/a2-religious-studies-meta-ethics.html

Metaethics: a brief summary

Metaethics is the study of ethical language. It differs from descriptive ethics (which is the study of what people believe and do ethically) and normative ethics (which is the study of how people make ethical decisions). Metaethics asks not 'What is good or bad?' but 'What are we doing when we are saying something is 'good' or 'bad'?' Metaethics raises questions about the ontological status and epistemological status of ethical statements. In other words, do ethical statements correspond with reality and is ethical knowledge possible?

Within Metaethics the main division is between 'cognitive' and 'non-cognitive' approaches. Cognitivism in ethical language means that an ethical statement is a proposition where it makes sense to enquire about its truth or falsity. A non-cognitive approach to ethical language is one where a statement is such where it makes no sense to enquire about its truth or falsity. Within cognitivism the main division is between realist and anti-realist positions. A realist position is one where ethical language conforms to reality in some way, either naturally or non-naturally. The two approaches within realism are 'Naturalism' and 'Non-naturalism' (also known as 'Intuitionism'). Naturalism has been variously characterised. Essentially it is the contention that ethical statements are propositions which are made true by objective features of the world, and that these moral features of the world are reducible to non-moral (natural) features of the world, and so ethical language outlines this relationship. For Aquinas his theory of NML tries to identify moral features of the world with human nature. For Bentham he reduced morality to feelings of pleasure. Other theorists, such as F. H. Bradley said what is 'right' is reducible to the extent to which one has conformed your actions and life to your place in society. Naturalism falls victim to the 'fact-value' distinction put forward by David Hume. We can, Hume thought, never cross the fact value distinction, for just because something is the case, by this fact it does not mean it should be the case. One can never cross the fact-value distinction without some further reasoning. In short, one cannot derive an 'ought' from an 'is.' G. E. Moore built on Hume's criticism of Naturalism to come up with the 'Naturalistic Fallacy.' The difference with Moore's version is that he says that 'good' cannot be reduced to a natural property such as 'pleasure.' This is because it is an 'open question' whether, for example, pleasure is good; the concept of goodness is not exhausted by pleasure in the same way the concept of 'triangle' is exhausted by 'three-sided shape.'

Moore's criticism of Naturalism then gave rise to his own realist position, which is known as Non-naturalism/Intuitionism. Moore's position was that good is a non-natural property which we 'intuit.' What 'intuit' means is not straightforward, for it is a mental process which is not the same as sensing, but it involves a judgement. Franz Brentano was an influence on Moore, and his 'intentionality' indicated that we can never perceive things in a value-neutral way, and that a well-ordered mind should be able to make a sound judgement on that which it perceives in this value-laden way. This gives some indication of the way in which Moore, who drew upon Brentano, understood intuition as a mental faculty linked to, but not reducible to, sensing, but which – of course-incorporated a judgement. By referring to a non-natural property, Moore hoped to keep ethics objective and real. By making the property non-natural he hoped to circumvent the is-ought problem and the naturalistic fallacy. J. L. Mackie was deeply critical of Intuitionism for he argued that this kind of non-natural property would have to be ontologically 'queer' (unusual) and knowable by some kind of moral sixth sense which we do not possess. Mackie's cognitivist anti-realist 'Error Theory' thought instead that morality is relative and does not correspond with reality, but that people erroneously think it does and so they are putting forward (erroneous) propositions when they make moral statements. Moreover, Bernard Williams (in *Morality*) noted that there are problems both with what Moore thinks we intuit and how we intuit it. Good does not function logically like yellow, for it pertains to attributes, whereas yellow sticks to its subject (one could be a good guitarist, but a bad human, whereas in a 'yellow duck', 'yellow' describes the whole being). Moreover, we do not have a moral sixth sense to intuit goodness. Therefore, Moore's Intuitionism cannot make ethical language meaningful. Ross put forward a different form of Intuitionism based on the prima facie duties. There are seven duties which we know 'at first sight' (*prima facie*) and we know by 'intuition.' None of these seven duties are more or less important than one-another, but we know to, for instance, prioritise 'fidelity' above 'non-malfeasance' in one situation, but not another. Ross' intuitionism suffers from arbitrariness; why are there seven *prima facie* duties and not more, such as 'worshipping God' for instance? What if two people have different intuitions in almost identical situations? Prichard was a final Intuitionist who thought we could intuit duties, rather than 'goodness'. He also thought that some peoples' sense of intuition could be more developed than others, which might account for possible subjectivity, although how we are meant to know whose faculty is more developed is another question and one without an easy answer.

Non-cognitivism has two main approaches: Emotivism and Prescriptivism. Emotivism's main proponent was A. J. Ayer. Given the influence Hume had an Ayer, it is not surprising Ayer applied this to ethics. Ayer's Emotivism flows from the problems he finds with cognitivism. For a statement to be meaningful, it has to be verifiable. This means it has to be analytically true (true by definition, such as 'A triangle has three sides') or synthetically verifiable through your senses. As ethical language falls into neither of these categories, then it cannot be meaningful and so cannot be propositional. However, ethical language exists, so what is it doing? Ayer concludes that ethical language expresses emotion. Although Emotivism is characterised often as the 'Boo-Hurray' theory, this was not Ayer's phrase, but Winston Barnes'. So if you do not like abortion, you might say 'Abortion is wrong,' but you are not proposing anything with truth value by saying such, but are instead saying 'Boo abortion.' C. L. Stevenson added to the theory by contending that emotions are based on opinions. Prescriptivism takes a similar point of origin but has a different take on what is happening when ethical statements are being made. R. M. Hare put forward Prescriptivism and held that while people are not making propositions with truth values when they are making ethical statements, they are trying to influence action by putting forward judgements which are universal, expecting all others to follow. In some ways this is not so different from Stevenson's form of

Emotivism for he held that these emotive statements are intended to influence the actions of others.

Issues arising from Metaethics

Whether or not what is meant by the word 'good' is the defining question in the study of ethics

This issue is difficult to resolve. To answer it depends very much on what you want from your ethics. If you are the victim in a hostage situation and you wondering whether you should lie to your captor, I doubt very much you will be contemplating the finer points of Metaethics—whether to adopt Ayer or Stevenson's version of Emotivism is likely to be far from your mind unless you are a philosophy major of a particular persuasion. Perhaps this take is uncharitable to the issue in question as it does say 'the study of ethics,' which is not the case if you are in a real-life situation. But perhaps this is part of the issue, that particularly Metaethics seems deliberately so far removed from the very business of making ethical judgements. As such normative ethics at least engages with outlining, explaining, and justifying different approaches of how to make ethical decisions, having practical relevance. Therefore, it could be said that the defining question in the study of ethics should be 'How do we decide what is good' rather than 'what the meaning of the word 'good.'' Nevertheless, in Metaethics' defence, there are significant implications for normative ethics of decisions made at the metaethical level. For instance, if it is decided that it is wrong to identify 'good' with 'pleasure' as Moore thought, then this has serious implications at the normative level for Classical Utilitarianism. Therefore, from an academic point of view it is probably correct to say that the meaning of the word 'good' is the most important question in the study of ethics, even if it is less than helpful in practical ethical situations. Perhaps this qualifier tells us- ironically- that something like Intuitionism is right as people often say they 'go with their gut' in difficult situations.

Whether or not ethical terms such as good, bad, right and wrong:

> **o have an objective factual basis that makes them true or false in describing something**

The divide here is between 'realism' and 'anti-realism' of its different stripes. The difficulty of relinquishing realism is that you end up in relativism or subjectivism. In which case, it makes it hard to support the strong ethical judgements people wish to make against issues such as 'racism' or 'genocide,' for who would want to say either of these issues could in some possible situation be ethical permissible or even right? This then leads us back into finding meanings of the terms 'good' or 'right' which have an objective basis, but then we are back with Naturalism or Intuitionism. However, in the summary put forward earlier in this chapter both theories had significant problems. One alternative is to say that ethical terms have a subjective factual basis according to the will of God. This is a cognitivist permission which means that ethical statements have a truth value, but according to this divine command position they rely on a subjective will—God's—but as he is meant to be omniscient, he knows everything and so his will is identifiable with the truth. This solves the issue of meaning that some actions can be seen as 'bad' and 'wrong' with certainty but not based on natural facts or intuitions, but on God's will. Of course, this depends upon faith in God's existence and so would not appeal to atheists and agnostics.

o reflect only what is in the mind of the person using such terms

The main approach this issue pertains to is Intuitionism. There is a sense of moral solipsism present in Intuitionism for there could be identical situations which admit of contrasting intuitions, with no mind-independent quality readily identifiable or impartial criterion at hand to adjudicate between people with contrasting intuitions. Intuitionism in some forms is meant to hold that there is some mind-independent quality which is real, but which is non-natural. However, given that this is only knowable through your mind, this makes it impossible to share with others in order to gain a contrasting opinion on the same phenomenon as there is no empirical referent for it. This is also going to be the problem with forms of non-cognitivism as they depend upon emotions in one's mind and body (Emotivism) and opinions in one's mind (Stevenson's version of Emotivism, Prescriptivism). Of course, Naturalists would disagree for they could point to positions in society (Bradley) or the human as a species (Aquinas) as sharable phenomena intelligible to others. Nevertheless, even with some naturalists, what counts as good, bad, right, and wrong is in their minds alone and not sharable with others, for feelings of 'pleasure' are subjective.

o can be said to be meaningful or meaningless

The meaningful/meaningless debate does not run neatly along cognitivist/non-cognitivist lines. Ethical language is meaningful to most cognitivists either as ethical terms refer to/are reducible to features of the world (Naturalism) or to non-natural, objectively-existing properties (Moore) or duties known with certainty (Ross, Prichard). However, Mackie was a cognitivist who thought that ethical language was objectively meaningless but he acknowledged that people the world over pretend that it is not. For non-cognitivists, ethical language is emotionally meaningful (Emotivism) and is practically important as it influences people (Prescriptivism), drawing upon the idea of the importance of 'speech acts.' However, non-cognitivism seems to make ethical debate meaningful as ethical statements are not propositions and so there is nothing to refer to or facts to discuss.

Whether or not, from a common sense approach, people just know within themselves what is good, bad, right and wrong

This issue clearly pertains to Intuitionism. The two main problems with this approach to ethical language are subjectivism and epistemological issues. The subjectivism problem is that what about people are who in the same situation but who have different intuitions, appealing to 'common sense' in both cases? It could be argued that, like Heraclitus, no-one can step into the same river twice and so there are no two identical situations, accounting for different decisions on the same appeal to 'common sense,' thus validating Intuitionism as a metaethical approach. However, in response I would argue that this is the case only in the trivial sense of different times, geographical places, and people; the moral issue is likely to be the same and so the decision is expected to be the same unless there are reasons or material facts which could justify a morally different approach based on a common-sense 'intuition.' The second issue is that of epistemology. What is a 'common sense approach'? How do we have it? Can it be wrong? This has major implications for responsibility, whether legal or otherwise. If common sense is infallible, this means that no-one can be wrong, which means that people cannot be blamed; it is almost the opposite of Kant's normative ethical approach which sets up a distinction between acting out of emotion or reason, with acting out of the former being neither morally blameworthy nor praiseworthy but acting out of reason being praiseworthy if followed through with a good will. The different with Kant's normative ethical approach is that he put forward a method with reasons for deciding upon how to act. Without conflating metaethics with normative ethics, the difficulty with Intuitionism is that where it does straddle the two kinds of ethics (normative and metaethical) it does so without explaining how the moral agent comes to their judgement, unlike Kant's approach, making it problematic for assigning praise or blame, concepts both of which are fundamental to morality. As for Moore's approach, both Williams and Macke pointed out the epistemologically 'queerness' of his approach, for how can a common-sense approach to ethics be based on something as mysterious as a non-natural property?

Sample essay

'Good is meaningful'- discuss (40 marks)

Every day we use terms such as 'good,' 'bad,' 'right' and 'wrong.' Although we use them in an unproblematic way, this belies a deeper problem of what it is exactly which gives these terms meaning. This metaethical problem is a difficult one, and it shall be argued that good is not meaningful in a cognitivist sense; it only has meaning insofar as it is a term expressing one's feelings of approval towards something, at the most encouraging others to do something.

My view, rightly, is that good cannot be a natural property as we cannot perceive it and it would have to be very strange. A. J. Ayer would say that good cannot be meaningful in this cognitivist, naturalist sense as statements involving the term 'good' are neither analytic (true by definition) or synthetic (verifiable through experience). When one hears 'Charity is good,' one can verify charity taking place as it has an empirical referent (the person giving to charity), whereas 'good' does not. Some philosophers, such as Bradley and Foot, would wrongly disagree, holding that the term 'good' has meaning insofar as we describe our right place in society (Bradley) or describing a function which helps us flourish as a good human being (Foot) and so by describing the empirically-verifiable human actions one is at the same time describing moral goodness, making ethical language synthetic and therefore meaningful. My view is more convincing as Bernard Williams has argued that what it means for a human being to be good (in role or function) is far more complicated and disputed than a cactus or a clock. As such, using the term 'good' to describe virtuous behaviour would be at best meaningful in a subjective way. J. L. Mackie would support Williams here in pointing to moral relativism as evidence that good cannot have any straightforward objective meaning. Moreover, Mackie's 'Error Theory' holds that humans wrongly think that ethical language is cognitive (where it makes sense to enquire about a statement's truth condition), whereas through relativism and the ontologically strange nature of 'goodness' as a moral property (where is it? How can we perceive it?), it makes sense to regard ethical language as non-cognitive. This means that ethical language is nothing more than an expression of emotion meant to indicate your approval ("X is good") or disapproval ("X is bad") of something. At most, as C. L. Stevenson thought, these emotions are meant to persuade other people into doing (or not doing) something, entailing that ethical language has emotion or perhaps even prescriptive meaning, but not objective meaning. G. E. Moore would not have drawn this conclusion, however, and thought that ethical language could be meaningful in a cognitivist sense through it referring to an objectively-real, non-natural property, and it is to this idea that we shall now turn.

My view, rightly, is that good cannot have meaning through being a non-natural property as it is ontologically strange and epistemologically unclear. What could a non-natural property be? Experience only tells us about natural properties. Also, how, with our physical, natural senses can we perceive a non-natural quality? If the nature and mechanism for acquiring an understanding of what is 'good' makes no sense, it cannot be meaningful. G. E. Moore would wrongly argue that ethical language is not meaningless as a well-ordered mind can intuit goodness in a situation with 'intentionality,' to use Franz Brentano's term. Moore's cognitivist, realist solution seeks to preserve objective meaning in ethical debates by appealing to the mind intuiting a non-natural property, avoiding the problems of Naturalism which he himself identified through his 'Naturalistic Fallacy.' To this end he is successful as he does not reduce goodness to a natural property; if, like Bentham, one said 'Pleasure is good,' Moore would reply 'X is pleasurable, but is it good?' By comparison, one could not say 'X is triangular, but does it have 3 sides?' However, my view is more convincing as by making goodness as simple and indefinable as yellow, Moore precludes meaningful ethical debate as what one intuits is subjectively known even if the judgements are meant to be objectively true. Moreover, Bernard Williams notes that there are problems both with what

Moore thinks we intuit and how we intuit it. Good does not function logically like yellow, for it pertains to attributes, whereas yellow sticks to its subject (one could be a good guitarist, but a bad human, whereas in a 'yellow duck', 'yellow' describes the whole being). Moreover, we do not have a moral sixth sense to intuit goodness. Therefore, Moore's Intuitionism cannot make ethical language such as 'good' meaningful.

Ethical language of good cannot be meaningful in an objective sense. This is because it cannot be verified and it is not analytically true, either. Although some naturalists have tried to point to a natural order of society or by reducing goodness to a function of human nature, Williams has pointed out that humans are more complex than this and people argue about what humans are and what is good for them, meaning it is not evident that 'good' has meaning by being reduced to human flourishing, status, or function. Moreover, whether goodness is a natural or a non-natural property, there are ontological and epistemological problems attached to these notions. As such 'good' can at most have subjective, emotive or prescriptive meaning.

Chapter 9: Sexual Ethics

Sexual Ethics revision summary

Key terms/ideas

- Goods of marriage
- Sacrament
- Fidelity
- Indissoluble
- Premarital sex
- Consummation of marriage
- Extramarital sex
- Cohabitation (contracts)
- Adultery
- Fornication
- Unitive sex
- Chastity
- Homosexuality
- Civil partnership
- Secularism
- Liberty Principle
- Negative liberty
- Positive liberty
- Harm Principle
- Apparent good
- Open marriage
- Permissiveness

Key scholars

Peter Singer, John Stuart Mill, Aquinas, Fletcher, Kant, Foucault, Bentham, W. Norman Pittenger, Augustine, Freud, Alan Wilson

Key quotes
'You shall not lie with a man as with a woman; it is an abomination' (Leviticus 18)
Story of Sodom and Gomorrah
'Malakoi' (male prostitutes) and *'arsenkoitai'* (sodomites) shall not enter the kingdom of God (St. Paul, 1 Corinthians 6: 9-11)—both words sometimes translated as 'homosexual'
'Image of God' (Genesis)
'Go forth and multiply' (Genesis)
'Love is patient' (1 Corinthians)
'One flesh' (Mark)
'There is neither Jew nor Greek, male nor female....all are one in Christ Jesus' (Galatians 3:28)
'Your body is a temple of the Holy Spirit…you are not your own' (1 Corinthians 6:19)
'It is better to marry than to be aflame with passion' (1 Corinthians 7:9)
'the social consequences of adulterous relationships were seen to be too damaging to be tolerated' (Anthony Harvey, *Strenuous Demands*)
'I know and am persuaded in the Lord Jesus that nothing is unclean in itself' (St. Paul, Romans 14)

Key documents
Wolfenden Report
Kinsey Report

Humanae Vitae
The Catechism of the Catholic Church
Issues in Human Sexuality
The Sexual Offences Act (1967)
UK Civil Partnerships Act (2004)
Marriage (Same Sex Couples) Act (2013)

Key case studies
Fletcher's 'patriotic prostitution' dilemma

Possible questions
To what extent are normative theories useful in what they might say about sexual ethics? (40 marks)

'Choices in the area of sexual behaviour should be entirely private and personal, not subject to societal norms and legislation'- discuss (40 marks)

To what extent do religious beliefs and practices concerning sex and relationships have a continuing role in the area of sexual ethics? (40 marks)

Curriculum links
- NML
- Utilitarianism
- Kant
- Situation Ethics
- Challenge of Secularism
- Conscience
- Freud
- Augustine

- Christian Moral Principles

Further reading
https://sexualethicsteachingresources.co.uk/

Sexual Ethics: a brief summary

Sexual Ethics includes many issues, from heterosexual and homosexual sex to sexual identity, masturbation, contraception, rape, adultery, pre-marital sex and more besides. The key issues are whether sex is a purely private matter or not, whether religion has any relevance anymore in sexual ethics, and where to look to resolve sexual ethical dilemmas.

Christianity is one source of moral authority for resolving sexual ethical issues. Traditionally, it has held that marriage is the proper place for sexual relationships (procreation, nurture, control of sex) for it is meant to be a stable relationship, which for Catholics is a sacrament. One of the primary purposes of marriage is to have children, and for Catholics they have said held that 'natural law...teaches that each and every marriage act [i.e., sex] must remain open to the transmission of life' (papal encyclical *Humanae Vitae*, para. 11). In other words, sex is to be unitive (for loving purposes) but must also intend to allow procreation. As procreation should be possible, traditional teachings are against homosexual acts, masturbation, and other types of sex which do not leave open the possibility of procreation. This is also found in the Old Testament, such as 'You shall not lie with a man as with a woman; it is an abomination' (Leviticus). Also, many Christians view the story of Sodom and Gomorrah as warning against homosexual sex. These same people are likely to believe that St. Paul as holding that homosexuals will not enter the Kingdom of God. Nevertheless, Christianity also holds more liberal teachings. The Church of England now permits 'trial marriage cohabitation.' For instance, Archbishop John Sentamu publicly supported Prince William and Kate Middleton's cohabitation as a sensible means of testing their desire to marry. As for members of the LGBTQ+ communities, Jesus supported the marginalised: 'let the oppressed go free' (Luke 4:18). At times over the past century (including still today in many countries), the LGBTQ+ communities are marginalised and so Jesus is on their side. As for St. Paul, some argue he was against male prostitutes, not homosexuality. Some people even argue that argue the infamous Leviticus text is against all kind of things we do not condemn today, such as making a garment out of more than one kind of fabric. Some clergy, such as CoE Bishop Alan Wilson, think that gay marriage enriches our concept of marriage.

Another approach to sexual ethical issues is Liberalism, which has developed over the last 500 years. It has firm tenets of individual liberty, equality of opportunity, free and open inquiry, free speech and debate, and humanism. It opposes totalitarianism, pseudo-science and censorship. Liberalism accepts that it will always be fighting unjust and oppressive powers and mediating between different ideas; it is open to, and encourages, debate. Everyone is equal in value under liberalism, and it accepts there is a universal humanity, and it is liberal assumptions which underpin the United Nation's 'Universal Declaration of Human Rights.' As such, it posits that there is a universal humanity, and also that individual humans matter and can differ in their beliefs and expressions of those beliefs. For journalist Edward Fawcett, the four themes of liberalism are 'acceptance of conflict, resistance to power, faith in progress, and respect for persons.' This respect for persons includes all people, which of course means that it is helpful for minorities such as LGBTQ+ people who have often been shown disrespect by the majorities in their societies. Liberalism is intrinsically goal-orientated, problem-solving, self-correcting and progressive. It accepts the scientific method, holds a correspondence theory of truth, and is based around reason, evidence, and empiricism. In the first half of the twentieth century, even to the 1970s, social justice causes were driven along liberal lines, including women's suffrage, black civil rights movement, and (relevant to sexual ethics) gay pride. John Stuart Mill articulated the Liberty Principle (sometimes called the 'Harm Principle') in *On Liberty*, where he argued that 'The only purpose for which power can be rightfully exercised over any member of a civilized community, against his will, is to prevent harm to others.' He put forward the notions of Negative Liberty (least state interference possible) and Positive Liberty (freedom to fulfil one's potential by being actively involved in government). Mill was of the opinion that tolerance makes for a happier society, which of course chimes with is Utilitarianism, and so he would have advocated that laws should not be in place to restrict sexuality if it is a purely private matter between people who are not doing harm to one-another and society more widely. Mill's liberalism was influential on Lord Wolfenden, who published The

Wolfenden Report in 1960 which was the basis for The Sexual Offences Act in 1967 which decriminalised homosexuality.

A further approach to sexual ethical issues is a postmodern one. Michel Foucault (1926-1984) was a French Philosopher who built his postmodern philosophy around the idea that 'knowledge is power'. While Marxists thought 'power' flowed top-down from the bourgeoisie (middle classes) to the proletariat (working classes), Foucault thought it flowed all around like a grid, and every exchange is a power exchange; how you experience power depends on where you are 'on the grid.' Although for Foucault power can come from everywhere, it can come from a 'discourse' (ways of constituting knowledge). If you reject the idea that there is any such thing as absolute truth, Foucault thought that all you would then be left with is what most people in a society at any one time decide is true (discourses). In other words, consensus dictates the moral agenda when it comes to what is normal and abnormal, natural and unnatural as far as human behaviour is concerned. From his study of history and the history of sexuality, Foucault found that what was regarded as perverted sexuality varied according to time and place, depending on who was in charge and got to decide on this. So, Foucault was an ethical relativist in this respect. For example, not so long ago, the power and influence of the Christian church was sufficient to ensure that homosexuality was regarded as unnatural, while more recently, psychologists like Freud and psychiatrists have been regarded as experts when it comes to deciding what is and what is not morally acceptable sexual behaviour. Foucault thought that all attempts to classify human sexuality in this way were misplaced and dangerous because they are designed to get people to conform to the moral standards of those shaping the discourse and marginalise those who fall into the abnormal category. Foucault believed that we should not allow our sexual behaviour to be dictated by what he referred to as these dominant 'discourses.' Foucault's ideas have been developed by his followers into what is sometimes called 'queer theory,' where the word 'queer' is intentionally used to question existing fixed views of sexuality. Foucault's ideas might be used to challenge the idea that any ethical theory might be helpful when considering matters of sexual ethics because that theory might simply be one of the dominant 'discourses' employed by a powerful group in society to pressure others into conformity or to marginalise people. And if we have bought into a 'discourse' by internalising as the voice of our conscience or super-ego (perhaps manifesting itself as guilty feelings around sex) then Foucault 's view of sexuality suggests that we should be questioning whether our conscience is reliable. When 'applied,' postmodern ideas can be seen to make more power flow from marginalised groups.

A final set of approaches would be to draw upon normative ethical theories to decide what is right or wrong with regard to sexual ethical matters. The OCR specification requires that you are able to apply Kantian Ethics, NML, Utilitarianism, and Situation Ethics to sexual ethical issues. With Kantian Ethics it is important to be able to distinguish between Kant's own personal prejudices (which were of their time) and the implications of his ethical theory. Kant's theory emphasises the importance of duty, universalizability, and not using someone as a means to an end. It also rejects emotions and emphasises the importance of reason in ethical decision-making. NML would place importance on the use of reason to act in accordance with ways which help us flourish as human beings in accordance with our God-given purpose, putting emphasis on reproduction, order in society, and defending innocent people in particular. Utilitarianism in its classical form would identify the good with maximising pleasure for the majority of people in the situation, although Mill's notion of a higher pleasures would downplay the importance of sexual activity (as it is a bodily pleasure) in favour of seeking intellectual, 'higher' pleasures. Preference Utilitarianism would give people what they prefer, not what makes them happy. Situation Ethics would advocate the most loving thing to do, even if it means disregarding laws of the land as it should put people at the centre of ethical decision-making.

Issues arising from Sexual Ethics

Whether or not religious beliefs and practices concerning sex and relationships have a continuing role in the area of sexual ethics

Christians would see religious beliefs and practices concerning sex and relationships as having a continuing role in the area of sexual ethics. Conservative Protestant Christians would look to the Bible for guidance, while traditionalist Catholics would continue to look to the Magisterium, Apostolic Tradition, and Bible for guidance. They would also likely search their conscience, too, for the right thing to do. Conservatively-minded Christians would likely see developments in sexual mores in liberal-minded societies as an irrelevance to what they should be doing. The early Christian theologian Tertullian wrote 'What has Athens to do with Jerusalem?' Augustine, too, might well have thought contemporary liberal and/or postmodern views and practices about, and concerning, sex and sexuality pertain to the 'earthly city' rather than the heavenly city. As such, traditional Christian views about the place of sex as limited to within a heterosexual marriage would likely still have relevance to anyone who thinks that anything other than an interpretation of God's will according to the sources of authority already mentioned would be irrelevant at best or morally evil at worst. Of course, liberals and postmodernists would see these conservatively-minded Christians as being out of touch or even dangerous. An extreme Christian group- the Westboro Baptist Church in America- have been labelled as a hate group and have even been banned entry to some countries for their homophobic views. Although there are some aspects of traditional, conservative Christian beliefs and practices concerning sex and relationships which are seen as intolerant or narrow-minded, there are other aspects which clearly can have a continuing role in the area of sexual ethics. One belief is the value of faithfulness to one's partner. This kind of faithfulness should also encourage people to keep promises elsewhere in their lives and so this can surely only be a good thing. Another beneficial aspect of Christian practices is the idea of procreation, for without it the human species would end. As Christians also believe in 'stewardship,' this, too, can be a useful belief to hold in conjunction with procreation to limit oneself to a responsible sized family keeping one's own finances- as well as the planet- in mind. Of course, another aspect to consider is liberal-minded Christianity. Liberal Protestants would keep both traditional sources of authority and human wisdom in mind when making moral decisions. As such they have adopted elements of secular liberal thinking making them much more open-minded to different sexualities. CoE Bishop Alan Wilson has even said that gay marriage enriches the concept of marriage than being merely to be tolerated. Arguably, then, liberal Christianity still has a lot to contribute to the continuing discussion of sexual ethics and relationship for it can bring to the discussion traditional values of faithfulness, practices pertaining to responsible procreation, and a celebration of diversity which resonates with modern secular liberal democracies.

Whether choices in the area of sexual behaviour should be entirely private and personal, or whether they should be subject to societal norms and legislation

Due to his Liberty Principle, Mill would have argued that sexual behaviour should be seen as a private affair and should be free of legislation unless it somehow impinged on others (the 'Harm Principle'). So, while Mill seems to be an advocate of the idea of choices in the area of sexual behaviour being private, he would not say they should be entirely private because sexual behaviour such as rape would harm others, so the choice to rape someone should be subject to societal norms and legislation. Mill's Harm Principle only applies to physical harm, however. Therefore, some people- such as Thomists- might think that something like homosexuality creates 'moral' harm to society in some intangible way, and so they would think that Mill's approach is wrong to take as it does not acknowledge harms in terms of standards, moral harm, and spiritual harm done by homosexual practices. Therefore, NML would judge choices in sexual behaviour to be something other than entirely private and personal, that one is accountable to God and should take 'order in society' into account. If you do not believe NML is plausible, however, then this would not have any purchase for you. Postmodernists, for example, would see NML as an oppressive discourse which has exercised undue power for centuries and so would reject it, seeing choices in the area of sexual behaviour as being entirely private and personal.

Whether normative theories are useful in what they might say about sexual ethics

Kantian Ethics is consistent, clear, and protects humans against sexual abuse such as rape as it is morally wrong to use humans solely as a means to an end, which of course would be the case with rape. Basing decisions off reason, not emotions, would stop the use of other people for reasons of 'lust' with one-night stands, pornography, or certain kinds of adultery. However, it is perhaps unrealistic to only act off reason as humans are embodied creatures and the post-Kantian philosophy has shown how implausible it is to act from 'reason alone.' On homosexuality, Kant had personal prejudices. Putting these aside to concentrate on the implications of his theory, Kant's theory is unhelpful if your starting point is the current status quo in a modern western liberal democracy, for universalising 'Have gay sex' would be a contradiction in the law of nature as if everyone followed the maxim there would be no-one around to perform the maxim as reproduction would not happen. Nevertheless, Kantian Ethics is helpful as you can universalise 'Respect differences in sexual orientation,' which chimes well with the modern secular liberal democratic value of 'tolerance,' which would help social cohesion. Postmodern thinkers would be sceptical of the Kantian value of 'reason' as it is seen as too monolithic a discourse which prevents the genuine acceptance of difference.

NML is seen as helpful as it is against any form of sexual violence due to the primary precept of 'Defend the innocent.' A secondary precept following from this precept is 'Do not sexually assault anyone.' This is helpful as it is a clear rule against sexual violence, underscored by reasoning which applies to everyone, with God's judgement to back it up. Perhaps less helpful today is the importance NML places on the primary precept of 'reproduction' as it restricts choices in sexual ethics (which is out of step with LGBTQ+ rights), downplays the value of using artificial contraception (which permits the spread of STIs), and could lead to overpopulation (which ironically goes against the primary precepts of 'defend the innocent' and 'order in society').

Utilitarianism is helpful insofar as its relativistic, teleological approach to sexual ethical issues permits diversity and tolerance, which accords well with a modern, liberal, democratic society. However, it does not do enough to prevent sexual violence. One can imagine a situation in which it could be in the 'greatest happiness for the greatest number' for a large number of people to take advantage of another person sexually. It could be argued that 'fecundity' and 'purity' would prevent this from being justified. However, the very fact that someone could use the Hedonic Calculus to try to justify sexual violence shows that Classical Utilitarianism is not sufficiently helpful to prevent sexual ethical abuse. Mill's notion of 'higher pleasures' also makes it unclear when it is ever morally right to procreate if 'competent judges' would (and should) prioritise higher pleasures to lower ones such as having sex. Preference Utilitarianism should in theory prevent sexual violence as you are meant to be impartial and put yourself in someone else's shoes, but this does not work if you were a sadomasochist. As such, Utilitarianism is not helpful. Nevertheless, Preference Utilitarianism is helpful for protecting animals as it against 'speciesism.' However, if Mill's 'Harm principle' is added into the equation, suddenly Utilitarianism becomes more helpful as there is some moral check on unrestrained harm to other people.

Situation Ethics has some of the same benefits as Utilitarianism insofar as it is relativistic and teleological, allowing diversity and tolerance with regard to different sexual ethical practices. In theory, 'personalism' should mean that unhelpful, old-fashioned laws and mores should be put to one side when doing the most loving thing. Relativism should mean that sexual practices can vary from place to place, which is helpful and does allow tolerance. However, this benefit can also be a drawback as there could be some ethical practices from other cultures which you would want to judge and prohibit, perhaps ones which allow for ages of consent to be too low. Furthermore, it has been said by some that Situation Ethics theoretically permits anything if it is judged to be the 'most loving' (which is arguably too ambiguous a concept); with sexual ethics, you would hope for a helpful theory to include more robust means by which you could draw a line in the sand and prohibit dangerous sexual practices.

Sample essay

Natural Law is the most reliable approach when making decisions about pre-marital sex. Discuss.

Natural Law is a deontological approach to ethics based on a teleological assumptions about what humans need to do in order to flourish. Pre-marital sex is sex before marriage. I will be arguing that Natural Law is more reliable than teleological approaches and other deontological approaches when making decisions about pre-marital sex.

My view, rightly, is that Natural Law is more reliable than teleological approaches when making decisions about pre-marital sex as Aquinas thought reason should lead you a clear judgement about what is right to do in each situation, avoiding you having to calculate possible consequences each time you consider having pre-marital sex. Aquinas thought as humans have the *synderesis* principle to 'do good and avoid evil,' humans would be drawn to do the right thing, and that reason helps humans to work this out by identifying the five primary precepts through which following them helps us to fulfil our purpose and achieve *eudaimonia*. Three relevant primary precepts here are 'reproduce,' 'live in an ordered society,' and 'worship God.' While it is easier to reproduce out of marriage rather than in it due to promiscuity compared with monogamy, 'ordered society' tells us that promiscuity is morally wrong, and that the security of marriage helps society be ordered. This is supported by 'worship God,' and this should make natural law dovetail with divine law, meaning humans should avoid 'fornication' and should instead aim for sex within marriage. A secondary precept, then, would be to avoid premarital sex. Use of reason should reliably indicate that premarital sex is wrong. Utilitarians such as Bentham would wrongly disagree with me, holding instead that maximising pleasure is the most reliable way to make decisions about premarital sex. This is because Bentham believe that pleasure is one of the two 'sovereign masters,' which guides humans towards happiness, by which he understood it as meaning pleasure. The Hedonic Calculus would be the guide here, especially when one considers a situation in which one does (long-term, unmarried relationship) or does not (one night stand) want a child, especially if one does not have any contraception; the Hedonic Calculus would help you consider the 'duration', 'purity' and 'extent' of the pleasure and it might be a more reliable way of making moral decisions as its flexibility helps you towards maximising pleasure in each instance. My view is more convincing as consequences are notoriously unreliable: a cohabiting, unmarried couple may think that a child will make them happy, but they might turn out to find parenthood very difficult. Two people in a one-night stand may think their contraception will work, but it breaks and the woman gets pregnant. By following Natural Law, these issues would not be problems as its reliable secondary precept against pre-marital sex would prevent couples entering into having children when unsuitable for marriage preparation ceremonies include talk about readiness for children, while one night stands are prohibited under NML as an 'apparent good,' not a 'real' one.

My view, rightly, is that Natural Law is more reliable to do with making decisions about pre-marital sex than Kantian Ethics as it does not depend upon one's interpretation of what it means to use someone as a 'means to an end.' As we have seen, Natural Law is clear and reliable about its position regarding pre-marital sex. Its adoption by the Catholic Church also provides further guidance insofar as one wishes to consult divine law, especially the Catechism of the Catholic Church. It is not reliant upon abstract concepts such as using someone as a 'means to an end,' and it takes society into account, not merely interpersonal relationships. Kant would wrongly disagree, holding instead that his duty-based, categorical imperative approach to ethical decision-making is more reliable as an autonomous self-legislator should be able to will as a universal law that premarital sex is wrong as one would be using the other person merely as a means to an end of their own gratification. As a universal law, one should be able to rely upon this in all situations when confronted with the ethical decision about whether or not to engage in pre-marital sex. My view is more convincing because it is unclear, and even implausible, that all situations of pre-marital sex involve one person using the other as a means to an end. While this might be the case regarding one-night stands, it is less likely when there are cohabiting, long-term couples who truly love one another and want to express their love for one-another through sex or to have a baby. As Natural Law considers both one-night stands and cohabiting couples, and has a clear, more plausible law regarding both (and is not reliant on deciding whether one is treating another solely as a means to an end), it is a more reliable deontological approach to making decisions about pre-marital sex than Kantian Ethics.

Natural Law is the most reliable approach to making a decision regarding premarital sex. As it is a rational, deontological approach to decision-making keeping a human's *telos* in mind, it is universally applicable to all humans. The *telos* of humans is not only individual, but also social, leading a rational individual to take not only reproduction into account, but also order in society and worshipping God, leading to a clear secondary precept not to engage in pre-marital sex. This is a clearer and more reliable than teleological approaches to the issue, such as Utilitarianism, which rely upon uncertain consequences to make a moral judgement. Furthermore, Natural Law is more reliable than other deontological approaches such as Kantian Ethics because it is embedded in a human's natural purpose and is not reliant upon an abstract interpersonal notion such as the second formulation of the categorical imperative, which could be interpreted different ways and not be clearly and reliably against (or for) all forms of pre-marital sex.

Appendix 1: A-Level Religious Studies Essay Advice

- Answer the question, not the general topic
- Evaluate throughout
- Juxtaposition is not enough
- Include small evaluative phrases
- Structure is important
- Length of answer is less important than answering the question
- Elegance of style is not rewarded, but clarity of expression is
- Relevant knowledge is important so long as it is being used to support the development of an argument
- Use evaluative phrases throughout: X rightly says...,' 'Y wrongly says...', 'X's view is more compelling than Y because...'

A-Level Religious Studies Essay Structure

Paragraph 1: Introduction, defining terms and signposting your argument (saying what you will be arguing).

Paragraph 2:
Start with your view, using a scholar/approach to illustrate it.

Counter your view with an opposite point of view, using a scholar/approach to illustrate it.
Say why your view is better than the opposing view.

Paragraph 3: repeat the structure of paragraph 2, but with different points.

Conclusion: summarise your argument (it has got to match what you signposted in the introduction and throughout).

Appendix 2: Evaluating how well an ethical theory applies to an ethical issue

There are four things to consider when evaluating how well a normative ethical theory (Kantian Ethics, Utilitarianism, Natural Moral Law and Situation Ethics) applies to an ethical issue:
1. The issue: **selecting relevant information** from the topic at hand, such as Euthanasia, Business Ethics, Sexual Ethics.
2. **Applying** the ethical theory *to* the issue.
3. Making a **judgement** on how well the ethical theory applies. To do this, you will need to know what different people might be looking for in an ethical theory. The best way to express judgements is through using adjectives/adjectival phrases, such as an ethical theory being described as:
    - Flexible
    - Morally right
    - Consistent
    - Up-to-date
    - Fair
    - Just
    - Easily applicable
    - Realistic
    - Cold
    - Humane

There are other criteria you could use.

4. It is important to **support your judgement**. It's no use saying that 'Utilitarianism is unjust' without substantiating why. If you have already mentioned when applying Utilitarianism that it aims to bring about the greatest happiness for the greatest number using the hedonic calculus, the injustice is implicit, but you need to draw it out and say exactly why the theory is unjust: allowing factory workers to be exploited because the goods they produce makes many more shareholders and customers happy is unfair on this minority of workers. To support your judgement, you may also choose to draw upon another scholar or ethical theory.

Here's an example from Business Ethics
Nike used sweatshops—*an aspect of the ethical issue (in this case, Business Ethics)*
My view is, rightly, that Kantian Ethics would say that it is always wrong to use sweatshops because, according to the second formulation of the categorical imperative, it is wrong to use a human being solely as a means to an end. In the case of Nike, they were using vulnerable children in developing countries solely as a means to an end of maximising profits for stockholders by producing goods more cheaply than in developed countries.—*application of theory (Kantian Ethics to the Nike case study).*
Kantian Ethics might not be sufficiently realistic, for although the children are being exploited, they are still receiving some money for their work, without which they might starve. If Kantian Ethics were more attuned to

feelings such as 'pain,' it might realise, as Classical Utilitarians did, that minimising pain and suffering matters.—*making a judgement on how well the ethical theory (Kantian Ethics) applies to the ethical issue (Nike case study), supported by some reasoning.*

Printed in Great Britain
by Amazon